Living in Asia, we see that (orld religion, teaches that men and women are equal in value and have the same life purpose of glorifying God and proclaiming him to the nations. But western culture has redefined equality as sameness, denying God's design and leading to the breakdown of churches and families. *Different by Design* is an accessible biblical theology of the God-ordained roles of men and women. In it, Carrie Sandom takes us from God's character, through creation and the fall, to Jesus and, ultimately, the new creation, showing us God's design for the sexes. Throughout the book, Carrie gives practical encouragements to live out our God-given roles, particularly in our families and churches, liberating us to be who God created us to be and inspiring us to do the work he created us to do. Males and females, whether single or married, will benefit from reading this book. May it help women, in particular, see the beauty and wisdom of God's design for our lives.

Keri Folmar

pastor's wife, United Christian Church of Dubai, United Arab Emirates
mother of three,
former chief counsel, U.S. House Subcommittee on the Constitution

Different by Design is an impressive outline of the Bible's teaching on the sensitive subject of gender. Carrie's faithful handling of the Biblical text and its application today combines depth and clarity with simplicity and grace. She argues convincingly that the differences between men and women go much deeper than the biological and, far from being oppressive, the complementary nature of their relationship is part of God's loving design for human flourishing.

Vaughan Roberts

Rector of St Ebbe's, Oxford and
Director of the Proclamation Trust, London

Different by Design traces God's specific design for men and women in the Bible from its revelation, rejection and masking, to its restoration in the lives of those who seek to apply it. With practical insights and scenarios, women especially will find this resource both biblical and culturally relevant.

—Margaret Elizabeth Köstenberger
author of *Jesus and the Feminists*
Adjunctive instructor of Women's Studies,
Southeastern Baptist Theological Seminary, Wake Forest, North Carolina

DIFFERENT BY DESIGN

God's blueprint for men and women

CARRIE SANDOM

CHRISTIAN
FOCUS

To Susie Fletcher and Heather Jackman.

Faithful servants of the Lord, who adorn the gospel of Christ and make it attractive.

'Consider their way of life and imitate their faith.'
Hebrews 13:7

Copyright © Carrie Sandom 2012

ISBN 978-1-84550-782-4

Published in 2012

by
Christian Focus Publications
Geanies House, Fearn, Ross-shire,
IV20 1TW, Scotland

www.christianfocus.com

Cover design by Paul Lewis

Printed by
Bell and Bain, Glasgow

CONTENTS

Introduction

Sally is thirty-five, highly motivated, fiercely competitive and, most of the time, happily single. She's a lawyer in a corporate law firm, and she's very good at her job. The senior partner keeps dropping hints that she should really think about becoming a partner in the next few years, something Sally would have jumped at not that long ago. But lately, and much to her surprise, she has started to wonder if this is really what she wants after all. Is this what her life will be about for the next thirty years?

Her father had always pushed her to succeed at school, and her teachers said she could achieve anything she wanted. Having a good brain and a good degree obviously helped, but she had also worked jolly hard for many years and fought tirelessly for recognition in her career. Although her current firm is an equal opportunities employer and promotes women as much as men, it still seems that the women have to work twice as hard to be trusted and taken seriously.

Whenever a female colleague leaves to have a baby, there is an air of mild frustration at the inconvenience it causes the rest of the team. And of course, if she doesn't come back to work but chooses instead to stay at home with the baby, everyone, women included, agrees that it is such a waste of a good and promising career.

Despite years of hard work and many late nights, Sally never considered for one moment that she would still be single at thirty-five. She had always thought that she would have a family as well as a career in law, the so-called dream of 'having it all'. But here she is, thirty-five and still not married. She enjoys the company of men and has been out with a few guys at church over the years, but the relationships have never really come to anything. She always remains on good terms with them afterwards, and they often confide in her for help and advice on how to approach relationships with other women. One man told her she was the older sister he'd never had, someone who could be relied upon to give him all the advice and wisdom he needed in navigating successful relationships with other women. Another remarked that she was one of the boys really – she had taken this as a compliment at the time, but wondered afterwards if any of these male friends would ever see her as an attractive woman instead of just a female friend.

Sally is just one of the scores of women I've met over the years who enjoys all the benefits of higher education and a promising career, but then, when life hasn't quite worked out as she hoped, has wondered if it's all been worth it. She can compete with almost anyone and come out on top, but maybe that's the problem. Her competitiveness, especially with men, has meant she's become almost untouchable – too competent, too skilled, too independent. She would dearly love to be married with a family, but that doesn't seem to be God's will for her life, at least not for now.

Not that the dream of 'having it all' is always able to deliver what it promises. Denise and Simon have been married for ten years and have two children. She works for a pharmaceutical company and travels the world marketing their products, while Simon is left to look after the children on his own. He works in IT and can usually work from home whenever Denise is away – although the children, especially when they were small, rarely allowed him to work as effectively as he would have liked. He found it hard being the only Dad at the church's toddler group and felt, at times, that Denise didn't give the children the attention they needed from their mother in those early years. He does what he can, but he can't be everything to them. He knows Denise's career has taken priority over his and, because she gets paid more than him, it seemed sensible to let that happen. But, at times, he can't help wondering what life would have been like if he'd married a less career-focused and more home-based woman instead.

Here in the West, the gradual feminisation of the workplace is indicative of the huge pendulum swing that has taken place in society over the last fifty years. Of course, the suffragette movement and the rise of feminism started much earlier than that, but many would say it is largely since the 1960s (and the availability of the Pill) that the biggest shift in the workplace has occurred. Women have more choice than ever before. They can choose what career to pursue, when to have children, and whether to come back to work full-time or part-time; government legislation in the U.K. has, by and large, made it much easier for them to do so.

These changes are not always bad in themselves but, collectively, they have had a huge impact on families, on society and perhaps, most crucially, on men themselves.

It seems that whenever there is a big pendulum swing in one direction to the benefit of some, there are those in the other direction who inevitably miss out. That's not to say that the feminist movement was entirely wrong. It rightly fought against institutionalised injustice, and I'm personally very grateful for the equal rights and opportunities I can enjoy as a woman in this country. I can vote, I can go to university and get a degree, I can travel almost anywhere on my own without arousing suspicion and, if the work I do is equally valid, I will get paid the same as men. Nevertheless, I do wonder if the pendulum has swung so far that we're now beginning to experience the backlash of an over-feminised and, dare I say, rather emasculated society?

Recently, I was travelling on the Underground when a heavily pregnant woman got into a very crowded compartment. Immediately, a young man in his twenties jumped up and offered her his seat. But in a loud and rather aggressive tone, she berated him for suggesting that she needed it. 'I can stand very well, thank you, and I'm rather offended that you think otherwise.' The poor man turned bright red, mumbled an apology and sat down, only to leap out at the next station. Whether it was really where he needed to get off or not, I don't know, but as soon as he was out of sight, the woman made a bee-line for his empty seat and sat down. Now why couldn't she just say 'thank you' and accept his offer of a seat? What did she think she was proving by refusing him in such an aggressive way? One thing's for sure, that man will never offer his seat to a woman again – and I am grieved by that. What has our society come to when a simple act of kindness is met with such savage hostility?

If women are on the front foot and in the ascendancy, then it seems almost inevitable that men are on the back foot and feeling rather vulnerable. Men today don't know whether they're supposed to walk on the outside of pavements, open doors for women, help them with their coats or offer to pay for drinks and meals on dates. If women in the West continue to assert themselves to the extent that they really don't appear to need men at all, then what role are men supposed to take? If they're not needed to care for and protect women, and are no longer likely to be the main bread-winner in the family, then what impact will that have on their masculinity?

Of course, the irony is that even though women are in the ascendancy, they end up being losers as well. The more passive men become, the more dominant women become, which means that, before long, strong male leadership will be a thing of the past. And when those strong assertive women want a strong assertive man to lead the family, take the initiative in the bedroom, work tirelessly in the same job for forty years and be the man they always dreamt of – well, there won't be any around! The growing feminisation of our society has had a devastating impact on the men it really needs.

But it's not just the workplace that is affected. Even our churches are becoming more feminised. The songs we sing are just one indication of this, as more and more choruses emerge with subjective 'Jesus is my boyfriend' language, rather than the objective truths of the Bible. Men find it hard enough singing out loud without having to sing as though they're teenage girls!

But the same process of feminisation is happening in the leadership of the church. As I write, General

Synod is debating whether women should be allowed to become bishops in the Church of England. The Biblical arguments against it seem clear and persuasive to me, but they are largely dismissed on the grounds that they're outdated and not suitable for our more enlightened society. I don't doubt that the equal rights argument will win the debate in the end, but somebody somewhere ought to do some research on what impact an over-feminised church will have on the church's mission to men. My suspicion is that where a church is led solely by a woman, most of the lay leadership will be female within five years, and the proportion of men in the congregation will steadily decrease. I would expect a similar trend to emerge if women were allowed to become bishops, with the number of men seeking ordination falling steadily in the years that followed. Men will be driven out of the church if women are too prominent within it and won't be drawn into it if men are too scarce.

The growing feminisation of our society has had a huge impact on the workplace, but it's our families and our churches that are feeling it the most. 'Having it all' may be the dream of many twenty-first century women, but there are others who question whether it's really what they want. Many conclude that it's not. Not when our desire to be treated the same as men means we're never really treated as women; not when our families are being run by highly competent, multi-tasking women, because the men have stopped competing with them and made a run for it; and not when our churches are great at drawing in women while the revolving door for men is as busy as ever.

Carrie Sandom
London

1

Different by Design

It was a Saturday night and I was travelling to Waterloo on the Jubilee Line (one of the rare occasions that it hadn't been closed for yet more improvement works). The compartment was almost full and the noise was quite overwhelming. There was a group of men at one end, celebrating another Chelsea victory in the Premiership, and a group of young women at the other, dressed to the nines and ready for a night out on the tiles. Beside me were two women talking about their earlier shopping spree on Oxford Street, and opposite me were three men who seemed to be talking about the various injuries they had inflicted on people in the past, whether accidentally or on purpose. Listening alternately to both conversations, I couldn't work out which was the more horrifying – hearing about the vast amounts of money spent on shoes in Selfridges or the gory details of a street fight in Aberdeen.

There's no getting away from it. Men and women are different. Different in the way they relate together (men with men and women with women), different in the way they spend their leisure time together, and different in the things they talk about. Every compartment of every Tube train on the Underground that night would have demonstrated these differences in one way or another. Men and women are different.

But what about in the workplace? Can these differences be seen there? Over the last twenty years or so, I have worked with men and women on a number of different teams – in Maths departments of secondary schools, on staff teams of larger and smaller churches, and on a number of different Christian camps for students and teenagers. My experience on all of these teams leads me to conclude that even in the workplace men and women are not the same.

You only have to listen to the way colleagues greet each other after the summer holidays to realise how different men and women are.[1] The men, if they greet each other at all, do so with a nod or maybe a slap on the back and a cursory 'Good break?' The women tend to greet each other with hugs and kisses all round, saying 'Hellooooo! So good to see you. Have you had a good holiday? How was your sister's wedding? Where did she go on honeymoon? How are your parents?'

So there's no getting away from it. Men and women are not the same, and problems arise when we ignore these differences and expect our friends and colleagues to be just the same as us! I once heard a vicar say that his life would be so much easier if only the women on his team could be just like him. Easier for him maybe, but terribly dull for everybody else!

---

1   I am grateful to the Rev. David Fletcher for pointing this out to me during my placement at St. Ebbe's Church, Oxford, in 1991.

MEN AND WOMEN ARE NOT THE SAME

The differences between men and women can be demonstrated in a variety of ways. For example, some people tend to look for satisfaction from their work, while others look for satisfaction from their relationships. These things are not mutually exclusive, but most people will gravitate towards one more than the other.

More task-orientated   More people-focused

This means that some people will be more 'task-orientated' and will focus on getting the job done, while others will be more 'people-focused' and concerned about the relationships involved in getting the job done. That's not to say task-orientated people aren't also relational, nor is it to say that those who are more people-focused won't ever get anything done! It's just that different people have different priorities and gifts. Some people will think that being task-orientated is more important than being relational and others will think the opposite, but you can't really compare the two that way. They are equally important qualities, and the Lord Jesus Himself perfectly demonstrated them both.

Now, at the risk of stereotyping these differences, it does seem that, generally speaking, men tend to be more task-orientated than women and women tend to be more people-focused than men. There are, of course, exceptions to this, but I'm talking in general terms. Even those who realise they are the exception to this will know that generally speaking the opposite is true for the majority of their sex.

So, men are the ones who will often have a ten-year plan, charting their expected career path, where they want to be, what they want to achieve and how they aim to achieve it. Women, by and large, don't have these kind of long-term plans and, generally speaking, don't think more than a year or maybe two years ahead. What plans they *do* have will be easily shelved if a significant relationship comes along – one with a husband, or a child, or a grandchild. I don't think there's anything wrong with this. It's indicative of their relational priorities but, sadly, I think there are some women in our churches who are exasperated by the men in their lives (whether fathers, husbands or friends) who insist that their daughters, wives and female colleagues need to have a ten-year plan! I'm not sure they do, at least, not in the same way as men seem to.

Waffles and spaghetti

Another difference between men and women is that, more often than not, men are able to compartmentalise their lives more easily than women. Phillip Jensen, the Dean of Sydney Cathedral, calls this 'the waffle and spaghetti factor'. Now, again, there will be exceptions to this, but, generally speaking, men seem to be able to compartmentalise their lives into a series of mental boxes – all neatly organised into rows, like the rows of squares on a waffle. They deal with things one box at a time and have a different box for the family, holidays, work, sport and so on. When they're at work, the 'work' box is brought to the table of their mind, the lid is off, and they concentrate hard on what's inside. At the end of the day the 'work' box is put back on the shelf with the lid firmly closed and they go home, where they deal with the 'family' box that is then opened and brought to the table.

Women, on the other hand, are more like a bowl of cooked spaghetti. The way their minds are organised means everything is interconnected with everything else. They can think about work, the family, their social life and what to cook for supper when they get home throughout the day. This doesn't mean they can't work effectively – their work will often be just as good as anyone else's – it just means they can think about more than one thing at a time. If the boxes analogy were applied to women, there really wouldn't be any need for shelves, because every box would be on the table and the lids would be off all the time!

The implications of these differences are huge and will be expressed in a range of different ways. To take an obvious example, waffle-minded men are able to switch off from their work much more easily than spaghetti-minded women. Similarly, the relationships men have with their colleagues will not tend to be as significant as the relationships women have with their colleagues. This means that women often get more emotionally involved with their work and take much longer to switch off at the end of the day. This explains why many women often need to talk through their day with someone – because talking about it helps them to switch off. Men, on the other hand, don't need to talk through their day in quite the same way, because they haven't invested as much of their emotional energy during the day and can easily move on to something else in the evening.

This also explains why people who are more task-orientated will often have a larger capacity for work than those who are more people-focused. They will tend to get more done, but they won't interact with the people they are working with very well. Those who are more people-focused will often get more emotionally drained by their work, and it will take them longer. They know the people they are working with much better and will spend more time deepening the working relationships they have with each other.

This means that men and women will often have different work outputs. Those who are more task-orientated will often get a lot done in a short space of time but, sometimes, someone will have to smooth over the relational mess that they have left afterwards! Those who are more people-focused will often anticipate the relational mess and avoid it, but it will take them longer to get the job done. And, if you think about it, you actually need both sets of skills if a team is going to be balanced and work together well.

Acquaintances and friends

Another discernible difference between the sexes is the way in which men and women develop relationships. Women often want to know significant information about their colleagues, such as where they live, the names and ages of their children, where they are going on holiday and so forth. But for many men, this sort of detail is just not that important. It doesn't mean they don't care for their colleagues or value them; they just don't need to know all this information about them!

I once remember telling a male colleague that after the meeting we were having I needed to go and buy a birthday present for one of the ministry trainees I was due to see that afternoon. He was completely astonished and asked, 'Why do you need to do that?' So I explained that if I didn't acknowledge her birthday in some way then she would feel I didn't care for her or value her. He exclaimed, 'I haven't a clue when the blokes' birthdays are but that doesn't mean I don't care about them or value them!'

And he was right. It didn't mean that he didn't care for the blokes on the team. But blokes and girls are different. I know that remembering the girls' birthdays is an important way of showing that I care for and value them. And forgetting to do so will communicate exactly the opposite, raising questions about the genuineness of the relationship we have – which for those who are more people-focused is crucial if the working relationship is to thrive.

Harsh words and negative criticism

This may also explain why women often find it hard to give and receive negative criticism. For them, negative criticism can devastate the relationship involved to the point that it will never recover. Now, undoubtedly, there are some women who are perhaps too sensitive about this, and they will need to learn how to handle criticism more positively. But a harsh word can irreparably destroy a relationship for a woman in a way that it doesn't seem to for a man.

I remember being part of a staff meeting where the assistant minister's sermon from the previous Sunday was being reviewed and critiqued. Some of the comments made by the team leader seemed to me to be utterly devastating, and I wondered if the relationship between them could ever recover. But here's the thing: the meeting came to an end, and within half an hour the two men were happily playing cricket with each other in the garden and then started rugby tackling each other. It seemed that the relationship had survived after all, despite the harsh words and negative criticism that were said less than an hour earlier. If those things had been said to me, I would have found it hard to know how the team leader could ever trust me to do anything ever again, but the assistant minister didn't hear them like that, and even though he managed to get the team leader in a headlock at one point, it was all very playful. At least, I think it was!

The point I'm trying to make is that those who are more task-focused don't seem to be affected by harsh words and negative criticism because, for them, the relationship isn't destroyed and remains intact. However, for those who are more people-focused, this kind of criticism can be totally crushing and the relationship will be destroyed. Understanding why people are affected by the same thing in different ways is important if teams are going to be managed and work together well. I fear it is not enough to tell those who are more sensitive that they just need to toughen up! You might as well ask them to jump over the moon.

Logic and intuition

Women are often more intuitive about people and can remember information about individuals that has long since been forgotten by others (like when someone's mother died), while men are able to think through something more logically and analytically. Again, there will be exceptions to this, but you rarely find all these qualities in the same person; the former are found more often in women, while the latter are found more often in men.

Here, then, are just some of the discernible differences between men and women. But how are these differences to be explained? Are they just cultural, or is there more to it than that?

Vive la différence!

Of course, some would argue that these gender differences are merely the product of our upbringing, the values our parents held and the type of school we went to. They maintain that if it were possible to put people into a different culture, with different values and different role models, the gender differences would likely disappear and perhaps even reverse. But others argue that there is more to it than merely how, when or where we were nurtured. So how are we to explain these differences?

Different bodies

Of course, biologically, there are the obvious differences. Men tend to be stronger, taller and heavier than women. Women are, generally, weaker, shorter and lighter. They are also affected by big hormone changes at various times throughout their lives, but tend to live longer than men. A man's initiative in fathering a child means that there is often a strong desire to protect, provide for and care for his family. A mother's bond with her child, especially in the first few months of life, means that she will often have strong nurturing instincts. Traditionally, these differences meant that the father became the main breadwinner of the family and found satisfaction in his work outside the home, whereas the mother stayed with the children and found satisfaction in her work inside the home. There's nothing particularly odd about this 'division of labour', although Western society today tends to view stay-at-home mums as rather lazy and unambitious! Shame on us.

Different brains

Some people go further than this and argue the differences physiologically. One book, '*Why men don't listen and women can't read maps,'* written by husband and wife team, Allan and Barbara Pease, argues that gender differences can be explained by analysing the male and female brains. Their research into how our brains have developed over the years leads them to conclude that an understanding of the differences between men and women is the key to all good relationships – and absolutely vital in marriage.

They trace the origin of our differences back to the hunter/gatherer era, and show how these different roles determined the way our brains have developed. Their findings explain why there are discernibly different skills and abilities between men and women. For example, they argue that men have enhanced long-range vision, because of the hunter in them, but find it hard to see things immediately in front of them (like butter in the fridge), while women have well developed short-range peripheral vision because of the need to protect their children from predators. This supposedly explains why modern-day women are generally not very good at judging distances in front of them and are more likely to run into the back of a car at a junction, while modern-day men are generally not very good at seeing cars coming from the left or the right and are far more likely to be hit by a car when they pull out!

Different by design

Now, there may be some truth in what these authors say, but, in my opinion, tracing back our differences to the hunter/gatherer era doesn't go back far enough. The differences between men and women are best understood theologically, because God's creative design is behind them. He is the creator and sustainer of the universe, and we are dependent on Him for everything.

From the movement of every muscle when we rise in the morning to the steady rhythm of breathing while we sleep at night, we are dependent on our loving heavenly Father, who designed us according to His good purpose and will.

While Adam and Eve were both made in the image of God and were therefore equal in status, dignity and humanity, they nevertheless had different roles in the Garden of Eden and within the family. They were equal in God's sight, but they were not identical. Adam was created first to tend the Garden and lead the family, and Eve was created second as his helper. But this helper role is not a derogatory role, despite what our twenty-first century sensitivities might tell us, as only with her creation is Adam able to fulfil his role of leadership. How and why God arranged things like this will be discussed in greater detail in chapter three. For now, it is sufficient to say that Adam and Eve had different but complementary roles, and each needed the other to play his or her designated part in God's plan. These *functional* differences do not confer either superiority on Adam or inferiority on Eve, and form the basis of God's blueprint for human relationships. Men and women are equal because they are both made in the image of God but they have different, and complementary roles.

One way of illustrating this complementarity is to think of a football team. The team has a shared aim (to score more goals than their opponents), but each member has a different role or function on the team and a different position on the pitch to achieve this aim. A team made up entirely of goalkeepers is not a balanced or complementary team and will have difficulty achieving their aim. A team where everyone wants to play attack will not defend very well. No one team member is more important than any of the others. They are equal in their *status* on the team, but they have different and complementary *roles* if the game is to be won.

The idea that men and women are equal but different is not at all popular in our society today. This is because society assumes that if two entities are equal, then they must also be identical. On this basis, the differences between the sexes need to be eradicated if equality is to be achieved. This is what brought the Equal Opportunities Commission into being and fuels the on-going debate on whether women should be allowed to become bishops within the Church of England (and no doubt archbishops in due course).

The long-running campaign for women to have parity in the prize money at the Wimbledon Lawn Tennis Championships serves as another example of this quest for equality. Up until 2006, the men's singles champion received more prize money than the ladies' singles champion. But in 2007, the ladies' battle for equality between the sexes was won and since then the men's and ladies' champions have received exactly the same prize money. Having achieved parity in one area, I wonder if the men will ever dare to suggest that if women are to receive the same prize money as them, then perhaps they ought to play five set matches as well!

EQUALITY AND DIVERSITY

If society's understanding of equality is very narrow, God's understanding of equality is quite different. For Him, it is quite possible for equality of status and diversity of role to exist alongside each other, without the implied superiority of one over the other. The Bible upholds the need for people to be treated with the same dignity and respect but allows for different roles without the implied loss of status – something our society finds hard to grasp.

These 'equal but different' characteristics are a reflection of God's own nature and being. There is one God, but three persons. Each person of the Godhead is equally God, and each shares the divine status; nevertheless each has a different role to play in creation, redemption and so forth. There is equality and diversity, unity and order at the very heart of the Godhead, and it is these qualities that are to be reflected in the way men and women relate to one another. Men and women are different by design. We are different ontologically – at the very core of our being – because we have been designed to reflect God's own nature and being. This is what it means to be made in the image of God. But to understand God's design for men and women we first need to understand the very nature of God Himself – which is what we turn to now in the next chapter.

DISCUSSION QUESTIONS FOR GROUPS/INDIVIDUALS

1. Who are the people you know who are very task-orientated? What do you admire about them?

2. Who are the people you know who are more people-focused? What do you admire about them?

3. How do the men and women in your workplace/family differ? To what extent do you think these differences are cultural? Is there more to it than that?

4. In what ways does our society seek to demonstrate equality by uniformity?

5. How can equality of status and diversity of role be better understood and embraced by Christian men and women?

2

The Pattern for God's design

Nancy had lived on the streets for years. Her husband had died some time before and when she couldn't keep up with the rent, she lost her home and all her belongings to the bailiffs. Her only option was to live on the streets by day and seek refuge in the homeless shelter by night. Being in a university town meant there were lots of students around who, perhaps being more aware of her plight than others, were open-handed with their gifts of food and money. She had lived off their generosity, friendless and alone, for four years.

My first encounter with Nancy was heart-breaking. I hadn't long been working at the church in the centre of this university town when she wandered into one of our Sunday morning services. She sat down at the back, murmuring softly under her breath. The years on the street had not been kind to her. Her hair was matted and flea-ridden, and she smelled terrible – having lived in the same clothes for many months. But, perhaps, the most pitiful thing about her was her inability to look anyone in the eye and the angry growl that greeted anyone who tried to engage her in conversation. She stayed until the end of the service, grabbed a cup of tea and a handful of biscuits when they were offered to her and shot out. We didn't think we would see her again. But we were wrong.

She started coming regularly. Always on a Sunday morning; always sitting in the same place, always murmuring softly to herself. She seemed caught up in her own little world and no-one could find a way in. She sat hunched up, often with clenched fists, and wouldn't let anyone talk to her. She waited patiently after the end of the service for the tea and biscuits to come, and then she was gone. At that stage we knew nothing about her, not even her name. Her inability to communicate effectively and her reluctance to let anyone close to her made it very difficult for any kind of relationship to begin.

But, then, one day, the church secretary bumped into her on the High Street. Without waiting for any reply, she said 'Hello. You're the lady who sits at the back of church on Sunday mornings. I've seen you a couple of times. I do hope we'll see you this Sunday. It would be so good to get to know you a bit.' And with that she walked on. Little did we know then what an impact that meeting would have.

She came the following Sunday and sat down in the usual place. But this time she was looking around, searching for someone. Well, it wasn't long before the church secretary spotted her and went to sit with her. She talked with her after the service over a cup of tea and learned that her name was Nancy. It's remarkable how knowing someone's name brings the potential for a whole new level of relationship – if, indeed, you could call the contact we'd had with her up until that point a relationship. It was as though this pitiful, dishevelled human being had suddenly become a real person.

It took a long time but, over the next few years Nancy changed beyond all recognition. She no longer growled at people and began to look them in the eye. Her whole physical demeanour changed as she grew in confidence, and she started to sit upright. Some of the social workers at the church managed to get her re-housed and, while her on-going health problems mean she will probably never hold down a regular job, she is off the streets and back in community. She loves to sing the songs and hymns at church and is learning to trust the Lord day by day. One of my most precious memories of her was the time she asked if she could take out a tray of tea and biscuits at the end of the morning service – so she could serve the church family in the same way that she had once been served.

Relationships and community matter. Without them Nancy had retreated into her own world and wouldn't let anyone in. The condition she was in when we first met her had almost dehumanised her. She lived on the streets knowing no-one and being known by no-one. I can't begin to imagine how terrifying that must have been for her. You see, we were made for community. A person is defined, in many ways, by the relationships he/she has with others – whether a father, mother, son, daughter, brother, sister or friend. But really, we shouldn't be surprised by this, because it is a reflection of God's own nature. He is both personal (in that we can know Him and relate to Him), and, He is in community and therefore defined, to a large degree, by the relationships He has within the Godhead (Father, Son and Spirit).

The whole of humanity is created in the image of God and has these same characteristics. We are both personal, with the capacity for relationship, and also made for community, where those relationships are defined and nurtured. Nancy has always been made in the image of God, but for a while that image had been terribly hidden – until she was known again personally and started relating to others in community. Where does this pattern for our design come from? It resides within the nature of God Himself. There is both individual personhood and corporate identity at the very heart of the Godhead.

ONE GOD, THREE PERSONS

The Bible is clear that there is only one God...

> Acknowledge and take to heart this day that the Lord is God in heaven above and on the earth below. There is no other. (Deut. 4:39)

> I am the LORD and there is no other. (Isa. 45:5)

> Is God the God of Jews only? Is he not the God of Gentiles too? Yes, of Gentiles too, since there is only one God, who will justify the circumcised by faith and the uncircumcised through that same faith. (Rom. 3:29-30)

And yet, the Bible also affirms that God is plural...

> Then God said, 'Let **us** make man in **our** image, in **our** likeness.' (Gen. 1:26)

> And the Lord God said, 'The man has now become like one of **us**, knowing good and evil.' (Gen. 3:22)

> Then I heard the voice of the Lord saying, 'Whom shall I send? And who will go for us?' (Isa. 6:8)

This plurality is explained by the three persons of the Godhead…

> 'Therefore go and make disciples of all nations, baptising them in the name [singular] of the Father, and of the Son, and of the Holy Spirit.' (Matt. 28:19)

> May the grace of the Lord Jesus Christ, and the love of God, and the fellowship of the Holy Spirit, be with you all. (2 Cor. 13:14)

> 'I (Jesus) will ask the Father, and he will give you another Counsellor to be with you forever – the Spirit of truth.' (John 14:16-17a)

It's important to understand that, while there is but one God, He is, nevertheless, three distinct persons. The Father is not the Son, the Son is not the Spirit, and the Spirit is not the Father. These distinct persons are revealed in a number of different passages in both the Old and New Testaments…

> In the beginning God created the heavens and the earth. Now the earth was formless and empty, darkness was over the surface of the deep, and the Spirit of God was hovering over the waters. (Gen. 1:1-2)

> The Spirit of the Lord is on me because the Lord has anointed me to preach good news to the poor. (Isa. 61:1)

> 'The Counsellor, the Holy Spirit, whom the Father will send in my name, will teach you all things.' (John 14:26)

> There are different kinds of gifts, but the same Spirit. There are different kinds of service but the same Lord. There are different kinds of working, but the same God works all of them in all men. (1 Cor. 12:4-6)

> In the past God spoke to our forefathers through the
> prophets…but in these last days he has spoken to us by his
> Son. (Heb. 1:1)

There is one God but three persons, and each person
of the Godhead is fully God. It may be hard for us to
understand how it is possible for God to be three in
one, but there is no doubt that God reveals Himself in
this way. He is one God (there is no other God but Him)
in three persons (Father, Son and Holy Spirit). What
is significant here is the nature of their status, their
function within the Godhead and the way they relate
to one another.

EQUALITY

The three persons of the Godhead may be distinct, but
Scripture teaches that they are equal. Each of them is
fully God, and this means they are equal in status. There
is no indication at all that God the Son is somehow less
God than God the Father, nor that God the Holy Spirit
is less God than God the Son. There are a number of
passages which illustrate this.

First of all, God the Father is clearly *fully* God. This
is evident from the very first verse of the Bible (Gen. 1:1
– 'In the beginning God created the heavens and the
earth'), but it is assumed throughout both the Old and
the New Testaments, in which God the Father is clearly
viewed as the sovereign Lord over all and the one to
whom Jesus prays.

Secondly, God the Son is *fully* God. The Apostle John
clearly affirms the full deity of the Lord Jesus Christ…

> In the beginning was the Word, and the Word was with God,
> and the Word was God. He was with God in the beginning.
> Through him all things were made; without him nothing

was made that has been made. In him was life, and that life
was the light of men. (John 1:1-4)

Here the Lord Jesus is referred to as 'the Word,' and
we're told that He was 'with God' and that He 'was
God' from the beginning. The Greek text echoes the
opening words of Genesis 1, which remind us that this
was true before the world was made. God the Son has
always been fully God.

The Apostle Paul similarly affirms that Jesus is fully God...

God was pleased to have all his fullness dwell in him.
(Col. 1:19)

For in Christ all the fullness of the deity lives in bodily form.
(Col. 2:9)

Thirdly, God the Holy Spirit is *fully* God. Once we
understand that God the Father and God the Son are
fully God, then verses mentioning all three, such as
Matthew 28:19 ('... baptising them in the name of the
Father and of the Son and of the Holy Spirit'), assume
the full deity of the Spirit, because they show that the
Holy Spirit is seen to be on an equal level with both the
Father and the Son.

Similarly, the Apostle Paul demonstrated his belief
in the divine nature of the Holy Spirit...

The Spirit searches all things, even the deep things of God.
For who among men knows the thoughts of a man except
the man's spirit within him? In the same way no one knows
the thoughts of God except the Spirit of God. (1 Cor. 2:10-11)

DIVERSITY
So, each person of the Godhead is fully God. They are
equal in status but each one has a designated role or

function within the Godhead. These different roles do not mean that one is more important than the others. The Father is not more important than the Son, neither is the Son more important than the Spirit – they are equal in status but different in function. This diversity can be seen in a variety of different contexts throughout Scripture.

For example, in **creation** we learn that God the Father speaks (Gen. 1:3, 'Let there be light…'); God the Son creates (John 1:3, 'Through him all things were made…'); and God the Holy Spirit brings life to all men (Gen. 2:7, 'He breathed into his nostrils the breath [literally, the spirit] of life, and the man became a living being'). The three persons of the Godhead are equally God but have distinct roles in creation.

Similarly, in **salvation** we learn that God the Father gives His Son (John 3:16, 'For God so loved the world that he gave his one and only Son, that whoever believes in him shall not perish but have eternal life'); God the Son substitutes Himself for us (1 Pet. 3:18, 'Christ died for sins once for all, the righteous for the unrighteous, to bring you to God'); and God the Holy Spirit breathes new life into the hearts of all believers, securing their entry into God's kingdom and marking them out as His people (John 3:5, 'No-one can enter the Kingdom of God unless he is born of water and the Spirit'; Ephesians 1:13-14, 'Having believed you were marked in him with a seal, the promised Holy Spirit, who is a deposit guaranteeing our inheritance…'). They are equally God but have distinct roles in salvation.

And again, in our **community life** together as the people of God: we pray to God the Father (Matt. 6:9, 'This, then, is how you should pray: "Our Father in heaven…"'); having been brought to Him through God the Son (John 14:6, '…no-one comes to the Father except through me'); while God the Holy Spirit intercedes on our behalf (Rom. 8:26, '… the Spirit himself intercedes for us with groans that words cannot express').

So, the three persons of the Godhead are equally God but they have different roles within the Godhead – demonstrated here in creation, salvation and the community of God's people, the Church – but there are other examples as well. These characteristics of equality and diversity lie at the very heart of the Godhead and form the basis of God's design for humanity. From Adam and Eve onwards, men and women have been made in the image of God and, similarly, are equal in status but different in function. If we ever doubt that equality of status and diversity of function can exist happily at the same time, then we should look no further than into the heart of God Himself.

But that's not all. The Bible reveals more about the nature of God in describing how equality and diversity work out in their relationship to one another. And we find that there is both unity and order within the Godhead.

UNITY

The oneness of God was at the very heart of the Israelite faith. For example, when Moses gathers the people of Israel on the edge of the Promised Land, he starts with an affirmation of faith…

> Hear, O Israel: The LORD our God, the LORD is one.
> (Deut. 6:4)

Jesus also affirms this truth when asked which commandment is the most important by one of the teachers of the law. He replies…

The most important one is this: 'Hear, O Israel, the Lord our God, the Lord is one. Love the Lord your God with all your heart and with all your soul and with all your mind and with all your strength.' (Mark 12:29-31)

But, as we have seen, Jesus also affirmed that He was God. So we mustn't think of God or relate to God as three separate beings or three Gods, but as one God in three persons. God the Son and God the Holy Spirit are clearly identified in Scripture as God, but in a way that doesn't compromise the oneness of God. God is one; He is united and indivisible as one.

Jesus actually affirmed the unity of the Godhead in a variety of ways. Consider these statements, all of them from Jesus, recorded in John's Gospel...

'I tell you the truth, the Son can do nothing by himself; he can do only what he sees his Father doing, because whatever the Father does the Son also does.' (John 5:19)

'I and the Father are one.' (John 10:30)

'But the Counsellor, the Holy Spirit, whom the Father will send in my name, will teach you all things...' (John 14:26)

'When the Counsellor comes, whom I will send to you from the Father, the Spirit of truth who goes out from the Father, he will testify about me.' (John 15:26)

'But when he, the Spirit of truth, comes, he will guide you into all truth. He will not speak on his own; he will speak only what he hears, and he will tell you what is yet to come.' (John 16:13)

Notice in the statements from John 14 and 15 that it is both God the Father and Jesus Himself who send the Spirit to teach and to testify. They are united in purpose as each member of the Godhead plays His designated role. So, God is one. He is united and undivided.

ORDER

But in addition to this, there is also order within the Godhead. This is perhaps the most neglected aspect of God's nature. While many agree that God is one, they often overlook the fact that there is also a definite order to the way the three persons of the Godhead relate to one another. Consider the following verses…

> 'For I [Jesus] have come down from heaven not to do my will but to do the will of him who sent me.' (John 6:38)

> 'And I will ask the Father, and he will give you another Counsellor to be with you forever – the Spirit of truth.' (John 14:16-17)

> '…the world must learn that I love the Father and that I do exactly what my Father has commanded me.' (John 14:31)

> 'But I tell you the truth: It is for your good that I am going away. Unless I go away, the Counsellor will not come to you; but if I go, I will send him to you.' (John 16:7)

> Now I want you to realise that…the head of Christ is God. (1 Cor. 11:3)

What's clear from these verses is that the Father exercises loving authority over the Son, who humbly and willingly submits to it; and both the Father and the Son exercise loving authority over the Holy Spirit, who similarly humbly and willingly submits to them. This loving authority neither confirms superiority on the one who exercises it nor inferiority on the one who submits to it.

Perhaps the most obvious demonstration of Jesus' willing submission to His Father is when He prayed in the Garden of Gethsemane the night before He died...

> He fell with his face to the ground and prayed, 'My Father, if it is possible, may this cup be taken from me. Yet not as I will, but as you will.' (Matt. 26:39)

> He went away a second time and prayed, 'My Father, if it is not possible for this cup to be taken away unless I drink it, may your will be done.' (Matt. 26:42)

> Going a little farther, he fell to the ground and prayed that if possible the hour might pass from him. 'Abba, Father,' he said, 'everything is possible for you. Take this cup from me. Yet not what I will, but what you will.' (Mark 14:35-36)

> He knelt down and prayed, 'Father, if you are willing, take this cup from me; yet not my will, but yours be done.' (Luke 22:42)

Here we see Jesus acknowledging His Father's authority, and at great cost to Himself, He willingly submits to it. There is both unity and order at the very heart of the Godhead.

BRINGING IT ALL TOGETHER

These four characteristics (equality, diversity, unity and order) are crucial to our understanding of the nature of God – Father, Son and Holy Spirit. All of them are true, all of the time. For example, consider these words of the Apostle Paul in his letter to the church at Philippi:

> Your attitude should be the same as that of Christ Jesus: Who, being in very nature God, did not consider equality with God something to be grasped, but made himself

nothing, taking the very nature of a servant, being made in human likeness. And being found in appearance as a man, he humbled himself and became obedient to death – even death on a cross! (Phil. 2:5-8)

Here we see that, although Jesus was in very nature God (unity), He did not consider equality with God something to be grasped (equality). Rather He humbled Himself, taking on the nature of a servant (diversity) and willingly submitted to His Father's will (order) by His obedience to death, even death by crucifixion. There was no battling for equal rights, He was one with His Father throughout. He accepted that He had a different function than His Father and willingly maintained the divine order by His humble submission to His Father's will.

It is these four characteristics – equality, diversity, unity and order – that form the basis of our design as men and women who are made in the image of God. We are individual persons, and distinct from one another, but we are nevertheless made for community and for relationship with one another. We are equal in status as the people of God but have different roles to play in God's world. We are defined, to a large extent, by the relationships we have with one another, and in certain designated contexts these relationships are to reflect the unity and order within the Godhead.

Nancy's tragic circumstances had dehumanised her. She knew no-one and was known by no-one. She had no community identity and, without being defined to some degree by the people around her, she had lost the ability to communicate. She never stopped being made in the image of God, but for a while she had lost the capacity to reflect that image in the world. Thankfully, that has now changed. She remains an individual in her own right, but she is now part of a community again; her community identity means that she is now defined to some degree by the people around her – people she can relate to; people she can talk to; people she can serve.

It is a huge privilege to be able to reflect God's image in God's world. But, as is often the case, with huge privilege comes great responsibility. Adam and Eve were the ones to whom God first gave the task of reflecting His image in this world. Their creation first revealed God's design for men and women. What that actually involved is the subject of the next chapter.

DISCUSSION QUESTIONS FOR GROUPS/INDIVIDUALS

1. How much do you think about God as Father, Son and Holy Spirit?

2. How significant is it that God is one in three persons?

3. Why do people find it so hard to believe that equality and diversity can exist at the same time?

4. How significant are unity and order in the Godhead? What would the alternatives look like?

5. Where should you look to understand the nature of your design? How does this challenge you?

3

The Revelation of God's design

His name was Bertie and Sarah loved him. But if anyone ever needed reminding that the created order is not as it should be, a few days in Sarah's house would have convinced them. You see, Sarah's house was Bertie's world and in Bertie's world, Bertie ruled. He had his own chair and frequently attacked people who sat on it. He was very demanding and insisted that his meals should be served before anyone else's. He positioned his bed at the bend in the stairs, in order to secure the greatest of vantage points. And if you ever tried to step over him, he would think nothing of sinking his razor sharp claws into your ankles, drawing blood more often than not.

Now I, personally, have nothing against cats – but then, not every cat is quite like Bertie. As far as he was concerned, Sarah was there to meet his every need. This meant that when Sarah and Graham got married and we reached that point in the service where the congregation was asked if they knew of any reason why the couple shouldn't be joined together in marriage, we all expected a loud '*miaow*' to be heard from the back of the church building.

Well, whatever battle you may be fighting with your particular pet, let me assure you that, in the beginning, God arranged things very differently. The two accounts of creation give us both a panoramic view as well as a microscopic one. Genesis 1 focuses on the broad canvas of creation while Genesis 2 zooms in on what happened when God made humanity. They are complementary accounts, not contradictory ones, as together they give us the complete picture of what happened when God created the heavens and the earth.

In recent centuries, Christians have disagreed about whether we should take the six days of creation literally, and it's not really my task to explore that issue here. However, Genesis 1 does seem to be written in order to teach us, primarily, about God's *purpose* in creation rather than the physical *process* of creation. Some people may find it hard to understand how the six days of creation can, literally, be six periods of twenty-four hours – especially when the sun isn't created until day four, but we must be careful not to relegate these accounts to mere symbolism alone. Jesus clearly believed that Adam and Eve were real people who were made in the image of God, and He quoted from these accounts when teaching His disciples about marriage.[1]

So, leaving aside the process involved, let's consider what we can learn about God's creation from these verses and what foundational principles they reveal about God's design for men and women.

---

1   See Matthew 19:1-6; Mark 10:1-9.

Order

In Genesis 1, God is the subject of nearly every verse or sentence. He is mentioned over thirty times and reveals Himself to be an all-powerful God who delights in good order; an order that is reflected in His own nature as well as His work. There is a repeated pattern of phrases throughout this chapter. 'Let there be...' is followed by 'and it was so...' and 'God saw that it was good...' is followed by '...and there was evening and there was morning, the first/second/third/fourth/fifth and sixth day.'

The first set of three days sees the creation of important habitats and the second set of three days sees the creation of just the right kind of inhabitants for these habitats. The table below summarises this.

Day	Habitat	Day	Inhabitant
1	Day and night (1:3-5)	4	Sun, moon and stars (1:14-19)
2	Sky and waters (1:6-8)	5	Birds and fish (1:20-23)
3	Land and vegetation (1:9-18)	6	Wild animals and livestock (1:24-25)

So, day and night are created on the first day as suitable habitats for the sun, moon and stars that are created on the fourth day. The sky and waters are created on the second day as suitable habitats for all kinds of birds and fish that are created on the fifth day. Land and vegetation are created on the third day as suitable habitats for different types of animals that are created on the sixth day. God makes them all out of nothing – all He has to do is speak, and it is so. God's powerful Word brings into being an ordered creation.

But that's not the only thing we learn here. God's creation has order but it also has...

Purpose

Bringing together a variety of birds, animals and fish is not the main purpose of creation. Amazingly beautiful and varied they may be, but God's zoo is not the main focus here. It is with the creation of humanity, which also happens on the sixth day, that we see God doing something much more significant. And the clue to this comes in the deliberate change in the pattern of the narrative...

> Then God said 'Let us make man in our image, in our likeness...' (Gen. 1:26)

It's a subtle but hugely significant change. 'Let there be' becomes 'let us make.' God reveals that He is plural (let *us* make) and humanity is created to reflect that plurality (*our* image, *our* likeness). None of the rest of the creation has been made in this way. The verse goes on, 'let *them* rule,' indicating that humanity is also plural. This means that individually we cannot adequately reflect God's image in His world, because to be made in the image of God necessitates being made in relationship with others, just as God Himself is in relationship with the other members of the Godhead.

But humanity is also made to represent God in His rule over creation...

> '...let them rule over the fish of the sea and the birds of the air, over the livestock, over all the earth and over all the creatures that move along the ground.' (Gen. 1:26)

This means that, in some sense, men and women stand in relation to creation as God does; as His chosen representatives, humans are the only creatures appointed to rule over the created order. This means that while dolphins and chimpanzees may be highly intelligent animals, they nevertheless do not have the task of ruling over the rest of creation – nor could they, because they are not made in the image of God.

The responsibility of ruling over the rest of creation is a delegated and not an absolute rule, as God Himself remains in charge. This is made clear in the way God commands His chosen representatives to…

'Be fruitful and increase in number; fill the earth and subdue it.' (Gen. 1:28)

The man and the woman may be rulers of God's world, but they are themselves subject to God's rule. This means that to be made in the image of God is to be made to *reflect* God by our ability to relate together, and to *represent* God by our capacity to rule. No other creature in the universe is able to do this. It is a privileged position that carries with it great responsibility.

God's creation has order and purpose, and lastly…

Blessing

If the purpose of creation is to reflect God's nature and rule, what does it all lead to? We find the answer to this question at the beginning of Genesis 2…

Thus the heavens and the earth were completed in their vast array. By the seventh day God had finished the work he had been doing; so on the seventh day he rested from all his work. And God blessed the seventh day and made it holy, because on it he rested from all the work of creating he had done. (Gen. 2:1-2)

The seventh day doesn't follow the same pattern as the previous six. There is no evening and morning at the end of the seventh day. Instead, God blesses the seventh day and then rests from His work – not because He is exhausted but because His work of creation is now finished. But this day of rest never ends. This means that the goal of creation, the point to which it has all been heading, is blessing and rest. God brings creation into being so it can experience His presence and enjoy the blessing of His good and creative work. This is what rest throughout the Bible involves – everything working together in perfect harmony, enjoying the blessing of God's presence and rule.

Everything is now set. God can leave His chosen representatives in charge of His creation. There is order, purpose and blessing. But, surprisingly, the creation account does not finish here. The rest of Genesis 2 focuses our attention more fully on the creation of the man and the woman on the sixth day.

GOD'S ORDERING OF HUMANITY

Adam and Eve are not created at the same time. They are both made in the image of God, in His likeness, but so that they can reflect the ordering of relationships within the Godhead, there is a designated order to their creation. God creates Adam first and places him in the Garden of Eden, the habitat created especially for him and his family.

> The Lord God took the man and put him in the Garden of Eden to work it and take care of it. And the Lord God commanded the man, 'You are free to eat from any tree in the garden; but you must not eat from the tree of the knowledge of good and evil, for when you eat of it you will surely die.' (Gen. 2:15-17)

God makes clear to Adam what life in the Garden will be like and what he is to do there.

Freedom and responsibility

Adam is to exercise his rule in Eden by working the Garden and taking care of it. There is both the development of the earth's resources and their right stewardship implied in these God-given instructions. This means that an important part of being made in the image of God is having the capacity to work. Work in itself is *not* a curse. It is a good thing and part of what makes us human. Anyone who has suffered the dehumanising effects of redundancy or not being able to work because of incapacity will know this.

With the responsibility of working the Garden, comes great freedom. Adam is free to eat from any tree in the Garden (and we can assume there were lots of them) – any of them, that is, except one. God's Word establishes the parameters for life in the Garden. If Adam chooses to eat from the tree in the middle of the Garden, the tree of the knowledge of good and evil, then he will die. It couldn't be simpler: 'Adam, if you want to enjoy life in the Garden then eat from any of these trees. If you eat from that one in the middle you will surely die.'

God's ultimate rule over creation means that freedom for His creatures is never absolute. It is always limited for our good. Just think for a moment about the fish in the sea. They are free to swim anywhere they like, but if they were to exert their independence and jump onto dry land, well, they would soon find out why their freedom is curtailed. Adam has a choice. He can choose to live in obedient relationship with His creator by eating the right fruit, or he can suffer the penalty of disobedient rebellion by eating the forbidden fruit.

But that's not all. The parameters that God sets out for life in the Garden mean that Adam has another important responsibility – that of leading the family. It's important to notice that, at this point, only Adam has been created, and only he is around to hear God's command about the tree of the knowledge of good and evil. He is the one who is responsible for warning Eve about eating fruit from this tree. He was created first and is God's designated leader. He must take responsibility for his family.

So, life in the Garden brings freedom and responsibility but it also brings…

Union and completion

There is work to be done, and we can imagine that Adam must have been eager to get started. But the rest of the chapter reveals that there is one last problem that needs to be addressed and only one way that it can be solved…

> The LORD God said, 'It is not good for the man to be alone. I will make a helper suitable for him.'
>
> Now the Lord God had formed out of the ground all the beasts of the field and all the birds of the air. He brought them to the man to see what he would name them; and whatever the man called each living creature, that was its name. So the man gave names to all the livestock, the birds of the air and all the beasts of the field.
>
> But for Adam no suitable helper was found. So the Lord God caused the man to fall into a deep sleep; and while he was sleeping, he took one of the man's ribs and closed up the place with flesh. Then the Lord God made a woman from the rib he had taken out of the man, and he brought her to the man.
>
> The man said,

'This is now bone of my bones
            and flesh of my flesh;
she shall be called "woman",
            for she was taken out of man.'

For this reason a man will leave his father and mother and be united to his wife, and they will become one flesh.

The man and his wife were both naked, and they felt no shame. (Gen. 2:18-25)

Verse 18 is supposed to stand out and shock us. After all the times God has surveyed His work and declared it to be good, here is a situation that is *not* good. It is *not* good for the man to be alone. He cannot adequately reflect God's image on his own, nor fulfil the creation mandate to fill the earth and subdue it. He needs a helper.

Now some people get very upset by this word 'helper,' thinking that it is a derogatory term and demeaning towards women. But we should remember that throughout Scripture, God Himself is described as the helper of Israel, someone whom they need and must come to rely on. Consider, for example, the following verses...

Moses said, 'My father's God was my helper; he saved me from the sword of Pharaoh.' (Exod. 18:4)

Blessed are you, O Israel!
Who is like you,
    a people saved by the Lord?
He is your shield and helper
    and your glorious sword. (Deut. 33:29)

But you, O God, do see trouble and grief;
   you consider it to take it in hand.
The victim commits himself to you;
   you are the helper of the fatherless. (Ps. 10:14)

Do not hide your face from me,
   do not turn your servant away in anger;
   you have been my helper.
Do not reject me or forsake me,
   O God my Saviour. (Ps. 27:9)

The LORD is with me; he is my helper.
   I will look in triumph on my enemies. (Ps. 118:7)

It's not that this helper will replace God in any way, far from it, but Adam needs a helper, a soul-mate, if he is to fulfil his God-given role, just as she will need him to fulfil her God-given role. There is both order and mutual dependence here. The role of helper is *not* an inferior one, nor is helper a derogatory term. It is a *unique* and *essential* role, as only with the provision of this helper is God's creation finally complete.

Nothing else God has made is able to take on this helper role. This is made abundantly clear as God first of all brings all the animals to Adam to see what he would name them. And it's Adam, not God, who has the responsibility of naming the animals – highlighting again that God has delegated to him the task of ruling over creation. An elephant lumbers along and Adam names him 'elephant'; a springbok bounces past and he names her 'springbok'! But none of the animals can fulfil the designated role of helper for Adam. So God causes Adam to fall into a deep sleep and makes a woman out of one of his ribs.

God could have made her from the dust, but instead He makes her from Adam himself – to show that she too is part of man (in the generic sense) and made in the image of God. One writer observes that the woman is not made from his head to rule over him, nor from his feet to be trampled by him. She is not made from his back to walk behind him or his knee to bow down to him. She is made from his side to stand by him, from under his arm to be protected by him and from near his heart to be loved by him.[2]

That might be a little over-sentimental, but it makes the point that Adam himself acknowledges in verse 23 – that she is part of him but also distinct from him. She is made of the same flesh as him but she is not identical to him. She is an individual in her own right but somehow also completes him. There is both independence and inter-dependence here. And Adam exercises his delegated rule once again by naming her 'woman' (literally 'out of man'), recognising that she came from him but is also distinct from him.

Verse 24 then defines the relationship that they will enjoy together. The verse starts with 'For this reason,' in other words, *because* woman was taken out of man…

> …a man will leave his father and mother, and be united to his wife, and they will become one flesh. (Gen. 2:24)

There is a deliberate ordering of events here – the man leaves his father and mother; he is united to his wife and then they become one flesh. The two are united as one – exclusively (he leaves all other family relationships behind), publicly (the union takes place in the presence of witnesses) and then sexually (they become one flesh in their bodily union). What's interesting here is that

---

2   Matthew Henry, *Commentary on the Whole Bible*, 6 volumes (Marshall Pickering, 1961).

their union is really more of a re-union of what had been one in the first place. Eve came *from* Adam but was brought by God *to* Adam in order to become one flesh *with* Adam.

It is a beautiful picture and perfectly illustrates that marriage is a lifelong commitment between a man and a woman that changes the focus of all other family relationships. It is a commitment with definite intention and starts with the man taking the initiative. It is to be witnessed by other members of the community and then consummated by their sexual union. He is to love and cherish her as his own body, because she is now a part of him. Similarly, she is to consider herself joined with him in loving partnership even though she remains an individual and distinct from him.

This is marriage as God intended: the coming together of a man and a woman, to form a one-flesh union that is broken only by death. This means we mustn't be naïve about same sex partnerships – they do not constitute a marriage. Scripture is clear that a marriage is between a man and a woman. We mustn't be deceived into thinking that pornography and masturbation are legitimate ways of satisfying our sexual longings. We cannot enjoy one-flesh union on our own. And we mustn't be fooled by those who say that sex can be enjoyed without making a public, life-long commitment first. The longing to be united in marriage and to become one-flesh with your spouse is God-given, but God also gives us the parameters for how those longings are to be satisfied.

Life in the Garden brings freedom and responsibility, union and completion. God's good gift of Adam and Eve to each other means that His work of creation is now finished. The wedding is over and life in the Garden can begin. We're then given a wonderful summary of their marriage relationship together…

> The man and his wife were both naked, and they felt no shame. (Gen. 2:25)

It's a picture of perfect harmony, of openness, acceptance and innocence. They are naked but not ashamed. This lack of shame is not a lack of conscience but rather an absence of any guilt – they have nothing to be guilty about. God's representatives are made to reflect His image in their relationship together and their rule over creation. Whether this means that if the Fall hadn't happened we would *all* have married we will never know. What we do know is that marriage is a wonderful gift, instituted by God and establishes the closest of all human relationships.

God's design for men and women

There is much for us to learn from these verses about God and His creation. But what do they tell us about God's design for men and women and how we are to relate together – whether within marriage or, more generally, outside of marriage? There are three foundational principles here. First of all, there is…

[1] Equality

God created men and women equal in status, dignity and humanity. They are both made in His image and both are needed to represent Him and reflect His image in His world. Men and women are both given the task of subduing the earth and ruling over creation. They are given to each other in marriage, the closest of all human relationships, where family life and the nurture of children are to be enjoyed as God intended.

Secondly, there is…

[2] Diversity

God created men and women with different roles in marriage. Adam was created first to lead the family and Eve was created second as his helper. This helper role is not the same as the leader role, but it is no less important. In order to be the leader God wants him to be, Adam needs Eve to help him and in order to be the helper God wants her to be, Eve needs Adam to lead her. Both are needed, but due to the order of their creation, Adam is the one who is ultimately responsible for their life together as a family.

Our natural tendency is to reject this ordering of relationships within marriage as unfair and unnecessary. But we need to remember that the ordering of human relationships is purely functional, as it is in the Godhead, and does not confer either a superior status on Adam or an inferior status on Eve. God the Father is head of God the Son[3] and God the Son submits to God the Father[4] – but they remain equal in deity. The way God has designed the very closest human relationship means that it is possible for equality of status and diversity of function to exist at the same time.

The third foundational principle is…

[3] Complementarity

If men and women are equal in status but different in function then, by definition, they are complementary entities. Not complimentary with an 'i' as in 'giving compliments to each other,' but complementary with

---

3   See 1 Corinthians 11:3.

4   See, for example, Jesus' submission to His Father in Gethsemane.

an 'e' as in 'bringing completion to each other.' This means that *on their own* they are to some degree incomplete. Now we need to be careful here. This does not mean that a single person is somehow sub-human or inferior. Neither does it mean that married people are super-human or superior. We would do well to remember that the Lord Jesus Himself never married while He was on earth, yet He perfectly reflected God's image in the world. He was also the most satisfied human being that has ever lived. What is clear is that, by definition, no-one can enjoy marriage on their own, nor can they enjoy on their own the complementarity that a husband and wife bring to each other. It is the closest of all human relationships. That is not to say that married couples have perfect relationships – far from it, but the marriage relationship is unique and cannot be experienced by one person on their own.

But we would do well to remember that marriage is not an end in itself; it is a means to an end. Because a marriage relationship is modelled on the relationships within the Godhead, husbands and wives have the responsibility of reflecting God's ordering of relationships in the world in a way that single people, on their own, do not. That is not to say that single people are entirely exempt from reflecting God's ordering of relationships in the world. The marriage relationship is used, in the New Testament, as a metaphor for the unique relationship Christ has with His bride, the church. This means that all Christians, whether male or female, married or single, enjoy the privilege of a complementary relationship with the Lord Jesus and, collectively, have the responsibility of reflecting that in the world. We shall look at this in greater detail later on.

Adam rejoices in Eve's likeness to him, and yet he is also thrilled that she is different than him. Adam is not given a mirror-image companion; he is given a woman, and he delights in her correspondence to him – which resides both in her likeness to him (she is human) and her difference from him (she is female). They are designed for one another. So, we are not to lament the differences between men and women. In the musical *My Fair Lady* Henry Higgins may have asked 'Why can't a woman be more like a man?' But that would be a disaster – we are meant to be different! We are meant to complement one another.

The closest human relationship is a marriage between a man and a woman where they are equal, but each has a different and complementary role. And these roles need to be exercised if God's ordering of their relationship is to be demonstrated effectively. They are in partnership together and need to work as a team, but neither of them can function effectively unless the other plays their part.

AFFIRMED IN THE NEW TESTAMENT

Equality, diversity and complementarity are the three foundational principles established at creation that give us God's design for men and women. And each of them is affirmed and upheld in the New Testament.

For example, Jesus affirmed the equality of men and women despite the prevailing Jewish and Roman cultures of His day. He spoke to women and expected them to relate to Him as individuals. He taught them alongside men and expected them to listen to His Word and be obedient to Him.

It is no accident that after the resurrection Jesus appears first of all to the women with the specific instruction that they should go and tell the disciples what they had seen – even though a woman's testimony was considered to be unreliable in Jewish and Roman law at the time. For more on this, see chapter six. The Apostle Paul similarly upheld the equality of men and women and taught that they are equally redeemed, equally adopted into God's family and equally marked by the Spirit.

The New Testament commends marriage as the norm for most people and affirms the diversity of roles for men and women within marriage. So a husband is head of the family and is to lead and love his wife sacrificially. And a wife is to submit to her husband, acknowledging that his leadership is God-ordained. We will be looking at this in more detail in chapter seven.

But the created order also has implications for the roles of men and women in the church family. So while Jesus certainly affirmed the ministry of women, He did not appoint them as His Apostles. Paul similarly saw the need to model the diversity of roles for men and women in the church and taught that only men were to be appointed as elders and overseers. That's not to say that women do not have a role to play in the life of the local church. Titus 2 seems to suggest that there is a role that *only* women can do, in the teaching and modelling of what it means to be a godly woman, but it is a role different from and complementary to the role of men. For more on this, see chapter eight.

Applied to the twenty-first century
But what are we to make of all of this? What do these foundational principles mean for us in the twenty-first century? Of course, some people pay no attention at all,

considering them out-dated and inappropriate for our more enlightened era, but I am convinced that while these principles were established at creation, God intended for them to be upheld in every generation. So what do they mean for us today? Here are a few suggestions...

The way we treat each other

Firstly, God treats men and women equally at every level, and we should do the same. We are made to reflect His image in our relationships and to represent Him on earth by our rule. And yet how easy it is to ridicule the opposite sex and put them down?

Some people would have us believe that women are in many ways superior to men – able to multi-task; able to have children and hold down a successful career; having a higher pain threshold and tending to live longer. Others would have us believe that men are superior – because they are stronger, taller and, generally, more detached and less emotional about their work. But the truth is, men and women are equal, and neither one is any more or less precious to God than the other.

God is not pleased when we despise, belittle or ill-treat the opposite sex. We mask His image in us when we do so. Being made in the image of God carries with it great responsibility. It is an honourable thing, and the way we relate to one another should demonstrate that. This means that we should repent of any ungodly attitudes or actions that we may have towards the opposite sex. For example, for not taking women seriously in certain professional contexts, or for thinking that men are hopeless and uncaring in certain domestic contexts.

More generally, we should treat *all* human beings equally. How easy it is to have a favourite child or a favourite parent and, yet, all of our children and both of our parents are made in God's image and equally precious to Him. How easy it is at work to get on well with some people (perhaps those with a similar ethnic background to us) but not so well with others – and to reflect that in the way we treat them or talk about them when they're not around.

How easy it is to dote on a young child but ignore the ageing pensioner. Why do people drive around with a 'baby on board' sticker in the rear window of their car? As if having a baby on board, as opposed to any other human being, should make us more careful on the road! Every human being, from conception onwards, is made in the image of God and has equal status, dignity and worth. Of course, the ethical implications of this are enormous.

The roles we have in marriage and the church

Secondly, God expects men and women to accept their diversity of roles in marriage and the family, and also in the church, which is God's family. If we want our families and our church families to provide a stable environment for nurture and growth, then we must let the men lead – that is the role that God has given to them. That's not to say that women have no part to play, but it may mean that, at times, we should actively hold back. Not in a way that leaves us biting our tongues and seething underneath, but in a way that gives men the time and space they need to lead. I sometimes wonder if our eagerness to help and be involved actually makes it harder for men to lead us.

A friend of mine said to me recently that after eighteen months of marriage to the most gorgeous

Christian man ever (that's her description, by the way, not mine!), he finally had the courage to say to her, 'You're the best wife I could ever have but please could you slow down on the good ideas as I don't have much time to mull them over before the next batch come.'

Another way of illustrating this is in the area of prayer. It's my observation that women are often very eager to pray out loud, but men are not and often hang back and just leave it to the women. Maybe it's just the churches I've belonged to, but women are often the ones who do the praying, whether it's leading the intercessions in church or praying in small groups or at the church prayer meeting. But I wonder if we held back a bit, maybe the men would be encouraged to pray a little more? That's not to say that women should never pray out loud, but I fear that our eagerness to do so can sometimes result in the men sitting back and letting us get on with it – but that's not good for them; in fact it's not good for us either!

But what if you've trusted in Christ and become a Christian since getting married and have a non-believing husband or wife? What if your husband doesn't see the need to lead the family in this way or your wife doesn't understand why she should submit? It can't be easy for people in this situation, and we should do all we can to support them. But the Biblical principles are there for *all* Christians, and we should do the right thing even if we cannot expect others around us to do the same. Of course, this means for those who are not yet married that marrying a non-Christian is out of the question; this is forbidden in Scripture anyway.[5]

---

5   See, for example, Exodus 34:15-16 and 1 Corinthians 7:39.

The secular workplace

But then some people are bound to ask, what about the secular workplace? To what extent should we model this diversity of role outside the family and the church? Is it permissible for women to hold leadership positions over men at their places of work? Some Christians think that the pattern established at creation should apply to secular work as well, but I'm not convinced that it should – because there are no covenant relationships involved in the secular workplace. God said in Genesis 1 that both male and female were created to subdue the earth and rule over creation. Other passages such as Proverbs 31 imply a degree of freedom in this area. We will be exploring them in greater depth in chapter nine.

It is therefore entirely appropriate for women to be chief executives, hospital consultants, head-teachers, team leaders and so on. But Christians in these jobs, whether they are male or female, need to be godly in the way they exercise these roles – demonstrating patience, kindness, goodness, gentleness and all the other fruit of the Spirit that should mark us out as different. My worry is that in order to be seen as adequate for the job, many women adopt a rather aggressive style in the way they work – which neither commends the gospel nor makes them very easy to work with.

So, we should treat each other equally and accept the diversity of roles God has for us in marriage and the church and rejoice in our complementarity. Men and women are needed to work together. We should embrace the fact that God has made us either men or women and that we need each other if we are to fulfil the creation mandate. Men and women on their own cannot adequately reflect God's image in the world or God's ordering of creation. We have an important part to play in demonstrating our complementarity – in marriage and in the church – and we will begin to fulfil our purpose in creation when we accept these roles and rejoice in them.

BUT WHAT ABOUT SINGLE PEOPLE...

Maybe, like me, you're a single woman, maybe you're a widow or a divorcee or a single mum, bringing up children on your own. What do these principles, if anything, have to say to us? Well, they teach us about marriage and what our role would be if God graciously gave us the gift of marriage. They help us to understand the sanctity of marriage and how to support our friends who are married. And I think they need our support and encouragement more than we imagine.

These principles tell us that marriage is for life and warn us, in fact they warn all of us, of the terrible consequences of being a marriage breaker. God hates adultery, and extra-marital affairs are off limits for Christians. We must not be naïve – single women, who are financially independent and seem to have a relatively uncomplicated life, can sometimes become very attractive to married men. We need to be wise! I've always made it a matter of principle when working with married men to ask them from time to time about their wives and their children (if they have any), and where possible to get to know their wives personally. I think it just helps to make the point that, as far as I'm concerned, the two of them have become one and nothing should threaten that relationship.

But I know that for some people reading this, the fact that you're not married is a cause of terrible heartache and pain. Many of the things mentioned in this chapter will have been agony for you to read and will have compounded the longing to be married and to become one-flesh with someone. Of course, we all have to live with unfulfilled longings – whether we are married or single. I know some single people find it hard to believe that but it is my observation that marriage doesn't change that. The unfulfilled longings may be slightly different but they are still there.

I believe the Lord wants to use these unfulfilled longings to teach us to depend more on Him and to cast our cares upon Him. He doesn't promise to take them away, at least not in this life, but He does give us the grace to live with them and to learn contentment in the midst of them. I have found it helpful, over the years, not to focus on the now but to keep looking forward to heaven. Some people only ever live for the 'dot' – the here and now, instead of the 'line' that goes on into eternity. So, we shouldn't focus our attention on the here and now, but need to keep looking ahead to the future.

This life isn't the real deal; the real deal is yet to come. The desire to be close to someone is a God-given thing and not to be despised. And, of course, it *will* one day be satisfied. Some of us will never marry, at least not in this life, but let's not forget that we are all heading towards the greatest marriage of them all – a marriage that will last for all eternity and will put every human marriage in the shade. So, as far as God is concerned no-one has been left on the shelf – we are all betrothed to His Son and He is the most wonderful bridegroom of them all.

DISCUSSION QUESTIONS FOR GROUPS/INDIVIDUALS

1. What aspects of God's nature and character are revealed in creation?

2. Why is being a helper not an inferior role for Eve?

3. How would society be transformed if God's parameters for sex and marriage were upheld today?

4. How should we demonstrate the equality, diversity and complementarity of men and women in (a) our families and (b) our churches?

5. How should we pray for (a) Christians who are married, whether to Christians or non-Christians, (b) Christians who are single and (c) for our children, in light of this passage?

4

The Rejection of God's design

In his book *Why men hate going to church*, David Murrow, an American TV producer, provides a series of reflections in an attempt to explain why American churches are failing to attract and keep hold of men. The observations he makes are very revealing and, sadly, all too common. Here, he describes a scene that would be typical in many of our churches.

> The pianist was just concluding the prelude as Judy slipped into her usual pew. Smoothing her crisp cotton skirt, she took her seat, exhaled deeply, and tried to prepare her heart to meet with Jesus. It had been a stressful morning.
>
> Her 12-year-old son, Matt, had refused to get up. He said he hated church and never wanted to go again. Judy argued with Matt, but the young man played his trump card: 'Why should I have to go to church if Dad doesn't?' In a moment of anger, Judy ripped Matt's covers off his bed and ordered the rebellious boy into the shower. She left his bedroom fighting back the tears.

Mark's attitude was beginning to affect his little brother and sister. All through breakfast they asked if they could stay home, complaining of mysterious stomach-aches. With Herculean effort Judy managed to get the three kids scrubbed, fed, and seated in their Sunday school classes on time. She won this battle but she was losing the war.

For years Judy had invested heavily in her children's spiritual development. Her kids rarely missed church. She volunteered in their vacation Bible school and Sunday school classes. She prayed for each child daily, and she rejoiced as, one by one, they invited Jesus into their little hearts. But now the children were turning their backs on the church, following the example of Judy's husband, Greg.

Greg. At that moment he was sitting at home in his pyjamas, remote control in hand. In their fifteen years of marriage he had attended church exactly thirty-one times: at Christmas and Easter each year, and the day they were married. Greg was a good husband and a great provider, but he was not the spiritual companion Judy longed for.[1]

Murrow goes on to explain why he thinks Greg is unlikely ever to go to church regularly. While some of his findings are more obviously tied to the American church scene, many of his observations can be applied to churches in the UK. I guess most of us will belong to churches that are heavily dominated by women and feel, very keenly, the lack of Christian men who can be good role models for the teenage boys in our churches. How many of our Sunday school classes are taught by men? How many of our youth groups? How many men are involved in discipling men or engaged in

1   David Murrow, *Why Men Hate Going To Church* (Nelson Publishing, 2005), p. 12

evangelising men? While there are some very faithful Christian men who are involved in all these things, it doesn't take them long to realise that they are usually heavily out-numbered by women.

WHERE ARE THE MEN?

So, where are the men in our families and in our churches? The typical twenty-first century man is often a far cry from the responsible, God-fearing and initiative-taking leader of Genesis 2. But, maybe, that's because the typical twenty-first century woman is often a far cry from the inter-dependent, God-fearing and team-completing helper that is envisaged there as well. It's not hard to see that godly, committed and wholehearted men are thin on the ground in our churches. But are we prepared to consider the possibility that it's the women in our churches who have driven them away?

In the previous chapter, we were left at the end of Genesis 2, with Adam and Eve about to start their married life together in Eden. God has created a world for them where there is order, purpose and blessing, and the parameters they need for life in the Garden are all in place. They have everything they need for a long, happy and fulfilled life together. So what happened? Where did it all go so wrong?

Genesis 3 can be divided into three scenes, in which Adam and Eve appear to be centre-stage but, we should note that, really, it is God who is the main character here. We continue to learn about God's rule and what happens when His chosen representatives rebel against it. We'll look at each scene in turn.

Firstly, scene one…

[1] God's Word ignored... leading to disobedience

> Now the serpent was more crafty than any of the wild animals the Lord God had made. He said to the woman, 'Did God really say, "You must not eat from any tree in the garden"?'
>
> The woman said to the serpent, 'We may eat fruit from the trees in the garden, but God did say, "You must not eat fruit from the tree that is in the middle of the garden, and you must not touch it, or you will die".'
>
> 'You will not surely die,' the serpent said to the woman. 'For God knows that when you eat of it your eyes will be opened, and you will be like God, knowing good and evil.'
>
> When the woman saw that the fruit of the tree was good for food and pleasing to the eye, and also desirable for gaining wisdom, she took some and ate it. She also gave some to her husband, who was with her, and he ate it. Then the eyes of both of them were opened, and they realised they were naked; so they sewed fig leaves together and made coverings for themselves.
>
> Then the man and his wife heard the sound of the Lord God as he was walking in the garden in the cool of the day, and they hid from the Lord God among the trees of the garden. (Gen. 3:1-8)

We are told that the serpent was more crafty than all the other animals, but we're not told why. What we do know is that he succeeds in reversing the order that God established at creation. God installed Adam and Eve as His chosen representatives and gave them the task of ruling over the rest of creation, with Adam being given ultimate responsibility. But in virtually one fell swoop the created order is turned on its head, with devastating consequences.

The serpent's tactics....

The serpent is wily and knows that to succeed in reversing the created order he must first of all topple Eve. And he targets her in three ways, each of them a challenge to God's supreme authority. His tactics are summarised by the table below.

Verse 1	Did God really say...?	He doubts God's Word
Verse 4	You will not surely die...	He denies God's judgment
Verse 5	God knows...you will be like Him	He distorts God's character

First of all, the serpent doubts God's Word. 'Did God *really* say you must not eat from *any* tree in the garden?' This causes Eve to question what God had said. The serpent then denies God's judgment by saying, 'You will not surely die' – which is a barefaced lie. No wonder Jesus described him as a liar and the father of lies from the very beginning. And, finally, the serpent distorts God's character when he says, 'God knows that when you eat of the fruit your eyes will be opened, and you will be like God, knowing good and evil' – making God out to be a killjoy and a spoilsport. These were the serpent's tactics in targeting Eve in the Garden, and they have been his tactics towards humanity ever since. Notice how rebellion against God's clear command is rationalised in the following example…

'Did God really say that sex before marriage is wrong?' We doubt God's Word. 'He wouldn't really mind, would He?' We deny His judgment. 'He knows that we love each other and He wants us to be happy.' We distort God's character. Every temptation to sin in some way doubts God's Word, denies God's judgment or distorts God's character – and sometimes all three. The serpent's tactics haven't changed over the years – but, sadly, our ability to resist him hasn't either. Let's see how Eve responds to all this.

Eve's downfall

First of all, Eve diminishes God's goodness and grace. God had said 'You are free to eat from *any* tree in the garden – except one' but Eve says here, 'We may *eat* from the trees in the garden but…' – the seeds of disobedience have already been *sown*.

Next, she exaggerates the prohibition God had given them when she says, '…but God did say, "You must not eat fruit from the tree that is in the middle of the garden, and you must not touch it, or you will die."' God had *not* said they couldn't touch the fruit, only that they mustn't eat it. Eve downplays God's goodness and magnifies His demands. By diminishing grace and exaggerating law, the seeds of disobedience are *well watered*.

And, then, she ignores God's Word altogether.

> When the woman saw that the fruit of the tree was good for food and pleasing to the eye, and also desirable for gaining wisdom, she took some and ate it. (Gen. 3:6a)

Notice that it is Eve's desire for wisdom and instant gratification that is her final downfall. She throws caution to the wind, rejects the created order, rebels against God's Word and gives in to her desires – the seeds of disobedience are *full-grown*.

The created order is partially overthrown and the serpent, a creature who was supposed to be ruled by God's chosen representatives, succeeds in his first conquest. He exercises rule over Eve. But all is not yet lost – surely Adam will intervene and save the day? But where exactly *is* Adam? The rest of the verse tells us…

> She also gave some to her husband, who was with her, and he ate it. (Gen. 3:6b)

There's no great battle for God's honour here! His chosen representative, the designated leader and head of the family, the protector and defender of God's rule, is overthrown in fifteen words, and he doesn't utter any of them! Eve, it could be said, at least entered into debate about the fruit, not that it did her any good in the end. But, Adam? He just takes the fruit and eats it.

Adam's downfall
Adam, too, rejects the created order and is ruled not by the Word of God but by enticement from his wife. Some have argued that perhaps he didn't know which tree the fruit had come from. But no! The passage says he was *with* her. The implication is that he had been present while all the debating had gone on beforehand but had said absolutely nothing. Adam abdicates his responsibility to lead in the marriage and allows Eve, his God-given helper, to take the lead instead. She reverses the created order and exercises rule over Adam, falling headlong into disobedience in the process. She then encourages him to follow her, which he duly does. This may explain why the serpent targets Eve as he does, not because she is more gullible than Adam but because she is the one who, in turn, can most easily influence him. It may be an uncomfortable thought, but it is nevertheless true, that the people we are most likely to lead into sin are the ones closest to us.

The immediate consequences of their disobedience are obvious. They realise they are naked and feel

embarrassment and shame for the first time, so they
hide from each other and make coverings for themselves
out of fig leaves. But they also hear the sound of the
Lord God in the Garden and feel fear for the first time,
so they hide from Him as well, seeking refuge among
the trees. It's a pathetic picture – and it's meant to be.
It's a far cry indeed from the harmonious relationships
they had enjoyed together at the start. But that's what
happens when God's Word is ignored and disobeyed.

Let's move now to scene two...

[2] God's Word upheld... leading to judgment

But the LORD God called to the man, 'Where are you?'

He answered, 'I heard you in the garden, and I was afraid
because I was naked; so I hid.'

And he said, 'Who told you that you were naked? Have you
eaten from the tree that I commanded you not to eat from?'

The man said, 'The woman you put here with me – she gave
me some fruit from the tree, and I ate it.'

Then the Lord God said to the woman, 'What is this you
have done?'

The woman said, 'The serpent deceived me, and I ate.'

So the Lord God said to the serpent, 'Because you have
done this,

Cursed are you above all the livestock
    and all the wild animals!
You will crawl on your belly
    and you will eat dust
    all the days of your life.

And I will put enmity
  between you and the woman,
  and between your offspring and hers;
He will crush your head,
  and you will strike his heel.'

To the woman he said,

'I will greatly increase your pains in childbearing;
  with pain you will give birth to children.
Your desire will be for your husband,
  and he will rule over you.'

To Adam he said, 'Because you listened to your wife and ate from the tree about which I commanded you, "You must not eat of it,"

Cursed is the ground because of you;
  through painful toil you will eat of it
  all the days of your life.
It will produce thorns and thistles for you,
  and you will eat the plants of the field.
By the sweat of your brow
  you will eat your food
until you return to the ground,
  since from it you were taken;
for dust you are
  and to dust you will return.' (Gen. 3:9-19)

God comes looking for them and calls out to Adam 'Where are you?' His rebellious representatives may have reversed the created order, but God is still sovereign. He quickly reaffirms that Adam is the designated leader of the family and calls out to him, in the first instance, rather than to Eve. Adam is the one who is responsible for explaining what has happened, although both of them are then called on to give an account for their actions. This is not done with ferocious interrogation but rather with a gentle and measured inquiry, as God gives both of them an opportunity to come clean.

Excuses, excuses

And that's when the excuses start. Both Adam and Eve are guilty of rejecting the created order, rebelling against God's rule and disobeying God's Word, but neither of them is prepared to accept responsibility for what they have done. Adam blames Eve, Eve then blames the serpent and the serpent? Well, he didn't have a leg to stand on!

But it's actually more sinister than that, because Eve isn't the *only* one whom Adam blames…

'The woman you put here with me…' (Gen. 3:12)

Adam even tries to hold *God* responsible rather than face his own sin, but God is having none of it. The LORD pronounces judgment on all three of them in turn, starting with the serpent. And in each case, God's judgment profoundly affects the essence of their existence and has both a present and a future dimension.

Judgment

God doesn't enter into any dialogue with the serpent but just condemns him. He curses him above all the livestock and all the wild animals. In the present, this means he will have to crawl on his belly and eat the dust of the earth. There will also be enmity between his offspring and Eve's offspring; and the battle with humanity will be fiercely fought in every generation. But, in the future, God's curse will lead to total and final destruction, as one of Eve's offspring will crush the serpent's head. The punishment for rebellion against God's rule is death, as God said it would be.

God makes it clear to Adam that there are two reasons why he is being punished…

> 'Because you listened to your wife and ate from the tree about which I commanded you "You must not eat of it"…
> (Gen. 3:17)

Adam stopped listening to God and listened, instead, to his wife, which meant he then disobeyed God's command about the forbidden fruit. Adam's punishment also has a present as well as a future dimension. In the present, he will suffer painful toil all the days of his life. No longer will he be able to rely on the fruit of the trees for food. Instead, he will have to grow his own. And it will be a sweaty business as the ground will produce thorns and thistles, making it jolly hard work. Providing for his family will be much more difficult now. In the present he will *work the ground* for food but in the future he will *return to the ground* in death, and will become part of the dust from which he had been taken.

Eve, too, will suffer the punishment of painful toil, only hers will be in childbearing. Family life will be hard work for her as well. The Hebrew literally reads, 'In your multiplying I will multiply your pain.' It is no accident that both the distinctive role Adam has as leader and protector of the family and Eve's distinctive role as child-bearer come under the same judgment. Both will now be hard labour and each will carry with it a degree of futility, as Eve, together with her offspring, will also return to the dust in death.

This means that both aspects of the creation mandate in Genesis 1, to fill the earth and subdue it, are affected directly by God's judgment. It will be hard to obey

God's command to fill the earth because childbearing will be so painful. And it will also be hard to obey God's command to subdue the earth because Adam and Eve's survival will be such hard work.

Ruined relationships

But these are not the only consequences Adam and Eve suffer as a result of their rebellion. Their God-given relationship together is also affected...

> 'Your desire will be for your husband, and he will rule over you.' (Gen. 3:16)

Not only will they battle with the serpent and his offspring, they will also fight one another. God gives them over to the consequences of their sin, and the battle of the sexes begins. Some people think that the desire stated here is a sexual desire leading to the sexual domination of men over women, but it is much more than that. This is not sexual lust; this is a lust for power. The same words for 'desire' and 'rule over' are used again in the next chapter when God warns Cain about the power of sin in his life...

> 'Sin is crouching at your door; it desires to have you, but you must master it.' (Gen. 4:7)

The words for 'desire' and 'master' are the same words in the Hebrew as the ones translated 'desire' and 'rule over' in Genesis 3:16. So, Eve will no longer willingly submit to her husband's lead and will seek to control and gain power over him instead. And Adam will no longer willingly exercise loving self-sacrificial leadership over his wife but will seek to rule over and master her instead. The loving primacy of Genesis 2 is now replaced by harsh rule. It's not a pleasant picture, but it comes as a direct consequence of their rebellion against God's design and order.

The battle of the sexes

This means that down through the centuries, women (who as Adam and Eve's offspring are born into sin and remain under God's judgment) have had a natural 'fallen' tendency to manipulate and control men, and the greatest expression of this will be seen in marriage – as they seek to manipulate and control their husbands. This also means that down through the centuries, men (who as Adam and Eve's offspring are also born into sin and remain under God's judgment) have had a natural 'fallen' tendency to either abdicate responsibility (which was Adam's sin in the first place) or else to dominate women abusively, and the greatest expression of this will be seen in marriage as they seek to master their wives. These sinful tendencies are not what God intended originally and come as a direct consequence of the Fall.

This battle of the sexes can actually be seen in all our relationships. As a teenager, I knew instinctively that if I wanted to stay out late at a party then the best way to achieve my objective was to ask my father, because I could get round him much more easily than my mother. It works the other way round as well, as boys instinctively seem to be able to get round their mums more easily than their dads.

But it's in marriage that the battle of the sexes is fought most fiercely, because marriage is the closest of all human relationships. Marriage as we know it is a far cry from the honest, open and harmonious relationship depicted at the end of Genesis 2, but that is a just and appropriate punishment for our rebellion against God's ordering of creation.

And so, finally, to scene three…

[3] God's Word sustained... leading to grace

> Adam named his wife Eve, because she would become the mother of all the living.

> The Lord God made garments of skin for Adam and his wife and clothed them. And the Lord God said, 'The man has now become like one of us, knowing good and evil. He must not be allowed to reach out his hand and take also from the tree of life and eat, and live forever.' So the Lord God banished him from the Garden of Eden to work the ground from which he had been taken. After he drove the man out, he placed on the east side of the Garden of Eden cherubim and a flaming sword flashing back and forth to guard the way to the tree of life. (Gen. 3:20-24)

God's ultimate purposes for His creation cannot be thwarted by rebellion and sin. While the created order suffers the consequences of Adam and Eve's rebellion, God's Word continues to rule, and even in the midst of judgment there is grace. It's worth noting that when judgment is pronounced on Adam and Eve, God does not curse them as He curses the serpent. He curses the ground instead of them.

The promise of a serpent crusher

The whole of creation is subjected to frustration on account of their rebellion, but Adam and Eve themselves are *not* cursed – it seems there is still some hope for them. And the basis for their hope is God's promise of a serpent crusher, one of Eve's offspring, who will crush the head of their crafty adversary once and for all.

Adam names his wife 'Eve', signalling a return to some semblance of order, and in doing so acknowledges the important role she will have as mother of the living.

God's grace to them means that in the short-term they will enjoy some sort of family life together, even while suffering the consequences of their rebellion against Him. The created order may have been rejected, but it is not completely destroyed.

But there is further evidence of God's grace here and indications that He has even greater plans for them.

The provision of clothes

We see this in God's gracious provision of clothes. The Lord gives them garments made of skin, indicating that blood needs to be shed in order to cover their embarrassment and shame. This is the faintest hint, perhaps, that in the future the death of another can make atonement for their sin.

Banishment from the Garden

God then banishes them from the Garden. His purity and holiness means that He cannot tolerate their wickedness and sin. If they were to stay in His presence He would have to destroy them – the just punishment for their rebellion. This means that their banishment is actually a loving thing even though it means Adam and Eve cannot live in His presence or enjoy the blessings of Eden any longer. God doesn't end their lives straight away; death and final judgment will come but in the meantime He graciously gives them time to work and enjoy life together as a family. It also means the search for the promised serpent crusher, one of their offspring, can get started.

Protection from eternal rebellion

God's grace is also seen in His protection of them. He guards the way back to the tree of life with a flaming sword so they cannot eat its fruit and become eternally sinful. This shows us that mortality is a blessing as it ensures humanity cannot live in rebellion against God forever. The tree of life doesn't appear again until the very end of the Bible where in Revelation 22 it brings forth fruit each month and provides healing for the nations. There is still an important role for the tree of life to play, but not while men and women are still sinful and suffering the consequences of their rebellion against God.

Genesis 3 ends with Adam and Eve banished from God's presence and fighting battles on two fronts – one with the serpent and the other with each other. But there has also been a monumental distortion of the foundational principles of our design as men and women.

[1] Equality ➔ Supremacy

Instead of equality, there is now a battle for supremacy. Instead of acknowledging that men and women are equal in God's sight, there is a fallen, sinful desire in all of us to be master of everyone around us. Women fight this battle by seeking to control and manipulate men. Men fight this battle by dominating women abusively or by abdicating completely (which is a way of getting women to do exactly the things they don't want to do!). These battles will emerge in a range of different contexts but they will be fought most fiercely in marriage.

[2] Diversity ➔ Uniformity

Instead of diversity, there is now a quest for uniformity. Instead of acknowledging that men and women have different roles to play in marriage and the church, there is a fallen, sinful desire in all of us to be seen to be exactly the same without any functional distinctions. Both men and women kick against the created order and reject the pattern for God's design. Diversity is seen as a weakness – a way of pandering to our patriarchal past. The result is a bland uniformity where gender differences are eradicated and despised, with everyone keen to be exactly the same as everyone else. What this means in practice is that we reject God's rule over our lives and either despise the distinctive roles He has given us as men and women or delight in them only when it suits us.

[3] Complementarity ➔ Conflict

And, lastly, instead of complementarity, where men and women appreciate the different roles they have and understand they need each other to fulfil them, there is conflict. Instead of the mutual respect and appreciation of our differences and the completeness that we can bring to each other, there is competitiveness, derision and distrust. Instead of enjoying the partnership of being equal but distinct entities there is a constant desire for power and control over each other.

This all came about because Adam and Eve disobeyed God's rule and ate the forbidden fruit! But that is what happens when we doubt God's Word, deny His judgment and distort His character. The rejection of God's order and design has serious consequences. Ultimately, of course, there is a quest for supremacy over God Himself, our loving creator. He made us in His image so that we might reflect His nature and represent His rule. But when we reject His divine plan we forfeit the right to enjoy equality, diversity, unity and order – those divine characteristics that we were designed to exhibit in God's world. By asserting our independence and, basically, telling God that He got it wrong and we know better, we have launched ourselves headlong along the road of broken relationships, pain, compromise, abuse, manipulation and chaos.

The battle of the sexes has been fought in every generation from Genesis 3 onwards, as the catalogue of relational disasters covered in the next chapter will demonstrate. Even in our churches, the battle has raged with some periods of history when men were in the ascendancy, to the detriment and exclusion of women; and, perhaps more recently (especially in the West) with women in the ascendancy, to the detriment and exclusion of men.

That is why Judy sits alone in her pew on Sunday mornings. She may long for the day when Greg stands next to her in church, holding her hand and singing praise songs with gusto; she may dream about how good it would be if they were ever to enjoy their morning devotions together; and she may long for the Christmas when, gathered around a sumptuous turkey dinner, Greg leads the family in prayer. Will he ever go to church with her?

Sadly, the answer to this question is very often 'no'. Not while she competes with him in the marriage; not while she does an excellent job in exposing his inadequacies and then showing how she can cover them up herself; not while he thinks church is for women and children and real men would never darken the door; not while he abdicates his responsibility for the family and leaves her to assume control of their children's spiritual lives.

When we reject God's order and design, the consequences are devastating and every aspect of our lives is affected. But, thankfully, because of God's goodness and grace, because of the coming of the promised serpent-crusher, not everything is lost.

DISCUSSION QUESTIONS FOR GROUPS/INDIVIDUALS

1. What are Satan's tactics in getting us to rebel against God's rule?

2. How is the battle of the sexes being fought today (a) in our families (b) our society and (c) our churches?

3. Where do we tend to fight the battle of the sexes most fiercely?

4. What evidence do we have of God's goodness and grace despite our rebellion against Him?

5. How should we pray for men and women in our churches, in light of this chapter?

5

The Masking of God's design

The consequences of our rebellion against God's order and plan are well documented. You only have to look at the newspapers to see how broken and chaotic our relationships have become. The following account is graphic and disturbing, but it serves to illustrate how twisted and manipulative relationships can get when people live without any reference to God.

Tori Dante was sixteen years old when her father raped her. It wasn't the first time. He had sexually abused her since she was six years old. What made this night different was the violence involved. In her frank and courageous book, *Our Little Secret*, Tori describes the terrifying events of that fateful night:

> After ten years of frequent sexual abuse, I was reaching the age when I no longer felt it necessary to quietly comply with his demanding behaviour. Until now I had managed to survive his assaults by blocking out all thoughts about what he was doing to me; I could, as it were, flick a switch

in my head and become totally impassive to him… For years I had felt powerless to do anything but now I was changing; I was not so afraid of him and I was prepared to challenge him.

The sound of him noisily opening my bedroom door woke me with a start. My heart started to beat wildly; moving quickly and defiantly he pulled the blankets off my bed. There was no soft talk tonight. No telling me to lie down while he gave me a 'cuddle'. Before I had a chance to get off the bed, he was on top of me. But the rising tide of fear made my reactions fast too. Sensing his anger; my courage rose to match. I don't know where I got the energy from but I pulled my legs back, put my feet on his chest and pushed him away as hard as I could. He fell backwards, lost his balance and landed on the floor.

For a moment he was dazed. But looking like a wild animal he came rushing towards me again. The resulting humiliation, coupled with my challenge to the emotional control he had exerted over me since I had been a little girl, sent him into an uncontrollable rage. He grabbed my wrists and dragged me from my bed along the landing to his bedroom. He flung me on to the bed and ripped off my nightdress. He shouted at me to open my legs and lie still. He wanted to take pornographic photos of me before continuing with his terror. I noticed his camera was already set up at the foot of the bed so he had been planning this, knowing we would be alone.

I refused to co-operate so he violently forced me to open my legs. I fought back. He held a pillow over my head to quieten me. I felt I was going to die. I thrashed about trying to gasp for air. It was hot. I couldn't breathe. I felt faint. I stopped struggling. Moving to his camera he shouted at me to open my legs. I heard the camera clicking. My strength started to return and I rolled off the bed and ran for the door but he had locked it. He caught hold of me again and flung me back on the bed. I started crying and screaming but he told me there was no point in making a noise – nobody was there to hear me. The house was in the middle of nowhere, he knew we would not be disturbed. So I stopped screaming and crying and instead begged him not to carry on. But he wouldn't stop. He pushed a vibrator into my vagina before turning me over and thrusting his penis into my anus. The pain was excruciating. My body went rigid with shock – I couldn't move. All my strength was suddenly gone; instead I was filled with utter panic. Could this really be happening? Could he really be this cruel and hurt me this much? Surely I was about to wake up and find I'd been having a nightmare. '[1]

It makes grim reading, but Tori's aim in writing so frankly is to help those who suffer abuse in similar ways; to help them realise that their mistreatment is unacceptable and there is a way out. But, wonderfully, she also writes in order to testify to the goodness and grace of God. Her remarkable story records how the Lord graciously rescued her from the all-too-common consequences of her abuse – the drug and alcohol addictions, the eating disorders, the promiscuous lifestyle and anti-social behaviour. Her faith in Christ and trust in all that He has achieved for her has helped her to come to terms with what happened, to trust in God's justice and receive from Him the strength to forgive her father for what he did to her.

Tori's abuse by her father was unimaginably awful, but it illustrates just one of the ways men have exercised excessive and unacceptable power and control over

---

1   Tori Dante with Julia Fisher, *Our Little Secret* (Hodder & Stoughton, 2nd edition, 2006), pp. 1-4.

women. Sadly, this kind of abuse is not that uncommon. According to statistics from the NSPCC (National Society for the Prevention of Cruelty to Children), published on The Lantern Project website, at least one child will die each week in the UK as the result of an adult's cruelty; 7 per cent of children experience serious physical abuse at the hand of their parents or carers during childhood; 1 per cent of children experience sexual abuse by a parent or carer and a further 3 per cent by another relative; 11 per cent of children experience sexual abuse by people known but unrelated to them.[2] A child whose mother is living with a partner who is not the child's father is thirty-three times more likely to be exposed to abuse than a child living with its natural parents who are married; every week 5,000 children suffer the pain and anguish of a broken home; 4,000 children call Childline every day.[3]

The evidence for the breakdown of family life is there for all to see. As one senior judge put it...

> All of society's social ills can be traced to breakdown of the family. In some of the more heavily populated urban areas of the country, family life is, quite frankly, in meltdown.[4]

And many politicians agree with him. In the Conservative Party election manifesto of 2010, David Cameron argued as follows:

---

2   Statistics from the National Society for the Prevention of Cruelty to Children, published on The Lantern Project website (www. lanternproject.org.uk, 2004-05).

3   Statistics published on the Good News Family Care website (www. gnfc.org.uk, 2009).

4   Mr Justice Coleridge, senior judge in charge of family courts in southwest England (April 2008).

Families matter because almost every social problem comes down to family stability. If we can get the family right, we can fix our broken society.[5]

But, of course, this is not a new problem. We can trace the breakdown of family life right back to Genesis 3 with Adam and Eve's rebellion against God's rule. The next chapter begins to spell out some of the ongoing consequences of that rebellion, as sibling rivalry leads Cain to murder his brother, Abel. God's comment on the state of humanity a couple of chapters later on is very revealing...

The Lord saw how great man's wickedness on the earth had become, and that every inclination of the thoughts of his heart was only evil all the time. The Lord was grieved that he had made man on the earth, and his heart was filled with pain. (Gen. 6:5-6)

The battle with sin rages in every successive generation, and as the descendants of Adam and Eve move further and further away from the Garden of Eden geographically, so marriage and family life move further and further away from the divine ideal revealed in creation. Here are just a couple of examples...

Abraham and Sarah

Abraham is undoubtedly a man of faith. Both the Old and New Testaments make that abundantly clear...

Then the word of the LORD came to Abram: 'This man will not be your heir, but a son coming from your own body will be your heir.' He took him outside and said, 'Look up at the heavens and count the stars – if indeed you can count

---

5   David Cameron (Conservative Party election manifesto, May 2010).

them.' Then he said to Abram, 'So shall your offspring be.' Abram believed the Lord, and he credited it to him as righteousness. (Gen. 15:4-6)

By faith Abraham, even though he was past age – and Sarah herself was barren – was enabled to become a father because he considered him faithful who had made the promise. And so from this one man, and he as good as dead, came descendants as numerous as the stars in the sky and as countless as the sand on the seashore. (Heb. 11:11-12)

So, Abraham was a man of faith, but he wasn't always the leader of the family as he should have been. Genesis records that, in order to get himself out of a jam, Abraham abdicates his responsibility to care for and protect Sarah, and instead passes her off as his sister – not once, but twice!

The first time he did this was during a time of famine…

Now there was a famine in the land, and Abram went down to Egypt to live there for a while because the famine was severe. As he was about to enter Egypt, he said to his wife Sarai, 'I know what a beautiful woman you are. When the Egyptians see you, they will say, "This is his wife." Then they will kill me but will let you live. Say you are my sister, so that I will be treated well for your sake and my life will be spared because of you.'

When Abram came to Egypt, the Egyptians saw that she was a very beautiful woman. And when Pharaoh's officials saw her, they praised her to Pharaoh, and she was taken into his palace. He treated Abram well for her sake, and Abram acquired sheep and cattle, male and female donkeys, menservants and maidservants, and camels. (Gen. 12:10-16)

Abraham's actions were not the greatest show of tender, loving protection towards his wife. But, wonderfully, the LORD vindicates Sarah and in order to secure her release inflicts all kinds of diseases on Pharaoh and his household. So Pharaoh returns her to Abraham and sends them away, with 'why didn't you tell me she was your wife?' ringing in his ears. Why indeed?

As if to add insult to injury, Abraham abdicates his responsibility as a husband and does exactly the same thing again a few chapters later. This time it's Abimelech, King of Gerar, who is deceived into thinking that Sarah is only his sister. The LORD graciously intervenes and rescues Sarah again, but when Abimelech calls Abraham to account for his actions, he offers this paltry excuse…

> I said to myself, 'There is surely no fear of God in this place, and they will kill me because of my wife.' Besides, she really is my sister, the daughter of my father though not of my mother; and she became my wife. And when God had me wander from my father's household, I said to her, 'This is how you can show your love to me: Everywhere we go, say of me, "He is my brother."' (Gen. 20:11-13)

There is something alarmingly Adam-like in this explanation, as Abraham even tries to lay the blame at God's door. If only He hadn't made Abraham wander away from home, none of this would have happened. Abraham may be Sarah's husband, but he abdicates the responsibility he has for her in an attempt to save his own neck. The LORD undoubtedly achieved great things in, and through, His servant Abraham but Abraham was far from a perfect husband. His marriage left a lot to be desired.

Jacob and the rape of Dinah

Jacob's family life was a disaster in so many ways. Tricked into marrying Leah when he actually wanted to marry Rachel, he ended up marrying them both. Together with his two wives and their servant girls, Bilhah and Zilpah, he fathered twelve sons and at least one daughter. But Jacob's family never enjoyed a happy home life. He favoured Rachel more than Leah and Rachel's two sons (Joseph and Benjamin) more than the others. The resulting rivalry and jealousy led to no end of problems and heartache, for all of them.

Dinah was Jacob and Leah's daughter. We know little about her except that she was raped by Shechem, the son of Hamor the Hivite, who ruled the area that Jacob and his family had settled in. She is overpowered, shamed and mistreated by a man who couldn't wait and forced himself on her. This is a far cry from the loving, tender and mutual one-flesh union that God had intended for marriage alone. Normally when rape occurred, it was the father's responsibility to vindicate his daughter and insist on some sort of recompense for her violation.[6] But Jacob abdicates his responsibility as a father and does little to support her...

> When Jacob heard that his daughter Dinah had been defiled, his sons were in the fields with his livestock; so he kept quiet about it until they came home. (Gen. 34:5)

Her brothers, on the other hand, couldn't sit back and do nothing. In perhaps their greatest show of solidarity, they unite to exact revenge on Shechem, but use excessive force in doing so...

---

6   See Deuteronomy 22:28-29.

Now Jacob's sons had come in from the fields as soon as they heard what had happened. They were filled with grief and fury, because Shechem had done a disgraceful thing in Israel by lying with Jacob's daughter – a thing that should not be done. (Gen. 34:7)

Because their sister Dinah had been defiled, Jacob's sons replied deceitfully as they spoke to Shechem and his father Hamor. (Gen. 34:13)

Three days later...two of Jacob's sons, Simeon and Levi, Dinah's brothers, took their swords and attacked the unsuspecting city, killing every male. They put Hamor and his son Shechem to the sword and took Dinah from Shechem's house and left. The sons of Jacob came upon the dead bodies and looted the city where their sister had been defiled. They seized their flocks and herds and donkeys and everything else of theirs in the city and out in the fields. They carried off all their wealth and all their women and children, taking as plunder everything in the houses. (Gen. 34:25-29)

The brothers' revenge is clearly a disproportionate response and goes way too far. The text makes much of their scheming and deception (something they had learned from their father, perhaps?) but Jacob's response to their actions is quite extraordinary, and further reveals his weakness as a father and a man...

Then Jacob said to them, 'You have brought trouble on me by making me a stench to the Canaanites and Perizzites, the people living in this land. We are few in number, and if they join forces against me and attack me, I and my household will be destroyed.' (Gen. 34:30)

Dinah had been mistreated and shamed, but here it seems that Jacob was more concerned about himself! The LORD God undoubtedly achieved His purposes through Jacob, not least in the provision of Joseph who later saved the whole family from extinction, but Jacob was neither a good husband nor a good father.

What's interesting about these narratives is the lack of any comment about these situations in the text, but surely we're meant to draw our own conclusions? Abraham's lack of protection for Sarah, Dinah's brutal rape and Jacob's weakness as a husband and father are all examples of how men abuse and mistreat women – sometimes by abdicating their responsibility to lead and sometimes by overpowering them with their sheer physical strength. But both of these tendencies come as a direct consequence of the Fall and are part of God's continuing punishment for sin. The cost of Adam's rebellion is far-reaching. A man's natural, fallen tendency to abdicate his leadership role or use it abusively, means that marriage and family life will be devastated in every generation. Once again, this is a far cry from the pattern God intended for men made in His image.

But, of course, women are also in rebellion against the LORD and pay little or no attention to His design for them as women. They are physically weaker than men and therefore have to resort to more subtle means. But they also fight the battle of the sexes very effectively and exert power and control over men in a variety of different ways, as the following examples show…

Samson and Delilah

Samson led the people of Israel for twenty years, during the time when God's people were ruled by judges. He certainly had his weaknesses and got himself into trouble with all sorts of women, but it was Delilah who exerted the most power and control over him. Persuaded by the Philistines to lure Samson into revealing the secret of his physical strength, Delilah really went to work. Maybe it was the money they offered her; maybe it was the thrill of playing games with him. Either way, she was very good at getting Samson to do what she wanted!

Her first approach was flattery…

> Delilah said to Samson, 'Tell me the secret of your great strength and how you can be tied up and subdued.' Samson answered her, 'If anyone ties me with seven fresh thongs that have not been dried, I'll become as weak as any other man.' (Judg. 16:6-7)

When the Philistines failed to subdue him by this method, she tried a little emotional manipulation…

> Delilah said to Samson, 'You have made a fool of me; you lied to me. Come now, tell me how you can be tied.' He said, 'If anyone ties me securely with new ropes that have never been used, I'll become as weak as any other man.' (Judg. 16:10-11)

When the Philistines again failed to subdue him, she tried a little harder…

> Delilah then said to him, 'Until now, you have been making a fool of me and lying to me. Tell me how you can be tied.' He replied, 'If you weave the seven braids of my head into the fabric on the loom and tighten it with the pin, I'll become as weak as any other man.' (Judg. 16:13)

But the Philistines failed to subdue him, so she played her trump card and nagged him endlessly…

> Then she said to him, 'How can you say, "I love you," when you won't confide in me? This is the third time you have made a fool of me and haven't told me the secret of your great strength.' With such nagging she prodded him day after day until he was tired to death. So he told her everything. 'No

razor has ever been used on my head,' he said, 'because I have
been a Nazirite set apart to God since birth. If my head were
shaved, my strength would leave me, and I would become as
weak as any other man.' (Judg. 16:15-17)

And this time she succeeded. Worn down by her
constant nagging, Samson gave in and, in a moment
of sheer exasperation, revealed the true secret of his
strength. She then lured him to sleep on her lap (why he
trusted her we will never know) and ordered a servant
to shave off his hair. The Philistines seized him, gouged
out his eyes and, binding him in shackles, put him in
prison. God's appointed leader was finally subdued – by
a woman! We hear nothing more of Delilah, but perhaps
there's no surprise in that. The mother of all nagging
wives had made her conquest and her work was done.

Herod and Herodias

Herod's weakness as a king is well-documented, but it
is the scheming of his wife, Herodias, that really takes
centre stage in this sordid tale. John the Baptist was
right to say that their marriage was unlawful. Herodias
had previously been married to Herod's brother, and
the law did not permit Herod to marry her while his
brother was still alive.[7] Because of this, Herod had
John arrested and flung into prison. Herodias nursed
a grudge against John and wanted to kill him, but she
was unable to because Herod, knowing John to be
a holy and righteous man, feared and protected him.
Finally, the opportune time came…

> On his birthday Herod gave a banquet for his high officials
> and military commanders and the leading men of Galilee.
> When the daughter of Herodias came in and danced, she
> pleased Herod and his dinner guests.

---

7   See, for example, Leviticus 18:16 and 20:21.

The king said to the girl, 'Ask me for anything you want, and I'll give it to you.' And he promised her with an oath, 'Whatever you ask I will give you, up to half my kingdom.'

She went out and said to her mother, 'What shall I ask for?' Her mother answered, 'The head of John the Baptist.' (Mark 6:21-24)

The sexual manipulation of men by women is a renowned and highly effective way of exerting power and control over them. After all the feasting and drinking, Herod may well have been slightly drunk – which would have made him even more vulnerable to the sensually provocative dancing. Whether Herodias' daughter knew exactly what she was doing or not, we will never know – but she certainly knew who to go to for advice about Herod's magnanimous offer. And Herodias was not going to miss an opportunity like that. She played on her husband's vanity, pride and foolishness in order to secure the prize she longed for: the death of John the Baptist.

At once the girl hurried in to the king with the request: 'I want you to give me right now the head of John the Baptist on a platter.'

The king was greatly distressed, but because of his oaths and his dinner guests, he did not want to refuse her. So he immediately sent an executioner with orders to bring John's head. The man went, beheaded John in the prison, and brought back his head on a platter. He presented it to the girl, and she gave it to her mother. (Mark 6:25-28)

Herodias succeeded in manipulating her husband into doing exactly what she wanted – even though it was against his better judgment. But her behaviour was a far cry from the gentle, affirming and supportive role God had designed her to have as a wife. The cost of Eve's rebellion is far-reaching. A woman's natural, fallen tendency to want to manipulate and control her husband means that marriage and family life will be devastated in every generation. This is not the pattern God intended for women made in His image.

OUR OWN GENERATION

All of this means, of course, that we will see the same battle being fought in our own generation as well. Men continue to abdicate their family responsibilities and refuse to take the lead as they should. The popular 'Supernanny' programmes on the television are a good example of this. The men in those programmes are often such wimps and do nothing to discipline the children, preferring instead to sit passively in front of the television and watch sport.

And all those teenage boys who roam the streets of our cities vandalising property and generally getting up to no good, who collect knife wounds as if they are badges of honour and think nothing of stabbing other people – where are their dads? Where are the positive male role models for them to aspire to? The whole of society is affected when men fail to take the lead in the family.

But women also play their part in this conflict. Because women are often so eager to show that they can manage without men, they stubbornly refuse to be in partnership with them and insist on doing everything themselves. When they realise that the men are hanging back and doing nothing, they nag them to do something, but then criticise their efforts and dismiss them as inadequate. Men need affirmation, not criticism – and constant nagging will drive them to inertia. Women may not be as physically strong as men, but they know how to manipulate and control them. Whether it's by alluring them sexually or harassing them verbally, women know how to exercise power over men. It's no wonder that the New Testament repeatedly urges women to exercise modesty in the way they dress and self-control in the way they use their tongues.[8]

---

8   See 1 Timothy 2:9-10, 1 Timothy 5:13 and Titus 2:3.

HOMOGENISATION

As our Western society seeks to become more egalitarian (in the sense of seeing everyone the same) there is an unhealthy homogenisation that not only masks the differences between men and women but even seeks to eradicate them. Wayne Grudem argues that different views on gender will inevitably affect other areas of life as well, as this rather provocative grid illustrates...[9]

View of...	The 'Effeminate' Left No differences	The 'Egalitarian' Left Deny many differences	The 'Complementarian' Middle Equal but different	The 'Domineering' Right Male dominance	The 'Violent' Right No equality
Men/ Women	Emasculation of men De-feminisation of women	No 'mars/ venus' differences	Men and women are equal but different	Men are better than women	Men as brutes Women as objects
Marriage	Same sex marriages approved	Mutual submission Husbands: wimps Wives: usurpers	Husbands: loving leadership Wives: humble submission	Husbands: harsh tyrants Wives: doormats	Polygamy approved
Children	Abortions justified as a rejection of a woman's role	Children raised with little discipline and little respect for authority	Children raised with loving discipline	Children raised with harsh discipline and little love	Female infanticide
Sex	Homosexual and lesbian sex approved Opposition to God's plan for heterosexual sex	Men become unmasculine Women become unfeminine	Monogamous sex Mutually-fulfilling intercourse	Pornography and lust Adultery approved	Violence against women Rape
Education	All single-sex schools prohibited	Systematic pressure to make boys and girls do equally well in all subjects	Boys and girls educated but different preferences, abilities and sense of calling respected	Boys given preferential treatment in schools	Girls prohibited from attending school

9 Wayne Grudem, 'Grudem's Grid: How different views on gender affect other areas of life' (published in *Evangelicals Now*, November 2000).

Grudem acknowledges that this grid has many gen-
eralisations and is only meant to show broad tendencies. He does not mean to imply that every person or
belief system within each column holds to everything
in that column. Nevertheless, he does show how a denial of gender-based distinctions impacts the way we
think about other areas of life and also reveals where
he thinks our Western society is heading.

Motherhood devalued

And it's certainly true that, with its quest for uniformity
rather than an acknowledgement of diversity, our society
often encourages women to ignore the unique role they
have as child-bearers (or at least to put it on hold) and
embrace a full and satisfying career instead. The desire to
be treated the same as men, and to enjoy all the benefits
of a long and successful career, means that motherhood
and family life are devalued and undermined.

It's not that women shouldn't have a career but
the care and nurture of children should take priority
over a woman's career because being a mother is more
important than where she works or how much she earns.
It is a role that women are physically, mentally and
emotionally equipped for, but are in danger of forsaking
because of the natural sinful desire women have to
compete with and be seen to be as successful as men.
We'll look at this issue in more detail in chapter nine.

There just aren't any women who, at the end of their
lives, say 'I wish I'd spent more time at the office.' More
often than not they regret not spending more time with
their children. Every mother I know regrets that to some
extent after the children have flown the nest but, those who
could have stayed at home and chose instead to further
their careers, are often the ones who feel most guilty.

This is also the case for those women who have terminated a pregnancy because it was inconvenient and didn't fit in with their career plans, who then have to suffer the mental anguish that always comes afterwards, especially if they cannot get pregnant at a more convenient time. Children are a precious gift from the Lord, and bringing them up to know and love Him is more important than where women work or how much they earn. Christian women in the twenty-first century need to recognise that we live in a society that doesn't value motherhood and in many ways positively undermines it. Family life is being eroded at every turn, and at the end of the day it is an expression of our rebellion against God's good design for us as women.

The Fall of humanity in Genesis 3 has had a devastating impact on all of us. We were born into sin, and all of our relationships are affected by it. Instead of order in the world, there is chaos – as the downward spiral of sin and rebellion takes its course. But even in the midst of all this madness, there is still hope. God's design for men and women was revealed in creation and rejected at the Fall, but it is wonderfully restored in Christ. The long-awaited serpent crusher has come and the effects of the Fall can now be reversed. The impact of His coming and the consequences of His victory over Satan are the subject of the next chapter.

DISCUSSION QUESTIONS FOR GROUPS/INDIVIDUALS

1. How did Abraham and Jacob fail their families?

2. How did Delilah and Herodias gain control over their husbands?

3. Where do we see the masking of God's design in our own generation?

4. How does our culture encourage us to rebel against God's design for men and women?

5. How should we pray in light of this?

6

The Restoration of God's design

In the summer of 1920, Dorothy L. Sayers was one of the first women to be awarded a degree from Oxford University. She had completed her studies some time before, but 1920 was the first year that women could actually graduate! Because of this she was often called a feminist, but she resented this idea and had no real political or social aspirations, either for herself or for women generally. She was a crime novelist and between the two world wars wrote over twenty books, all of them featuring Peter Wimsey, an amateur sleuth who was to become her most famous character. But, as a strong believer in the Lord Jesus Christ, she also wrote books and essays commenting on various issues from a Christian point of view. Despite her popularity as a crime novelist, her Christian writings were often met with cynicism and derision.

One such essay raised the issue of how women were maligned and mistreated by men. She was not a political animal but, nevertheless, saw the need to raise questions about the endemic male chauvinism of British society. She observed that the way men treat women is often an indication of how much (or how little) they value them – and maintained that, in the Lord Jesus Christ, women will find the *perfect* man, who treats them well because He values them so much. This is what she wrote about Him...

> Perhaps it is no wonder that women were first at the manger and last at the cross. They had never known a man like this man. There has never been another. A prophet and a teacher who never nagged them, never flattered or coaxed or patronised them; who never made jokes about them and never treated them as either 'The women, God help us!' or 'The ladies, God bless them!'; a man who rebuked without destroying and praised without condescension; who took their questions and comments seriously; who never urged them to become more feminine or jeered at them for being female; who had no axe to grind and no uneasy male dignity to defend; who took them as He found them and was completely unselfconscious in His relationships with them. There is no act, no sermon, no parable in any of the gospels that borrows its pungency from female perversity; nobody could possibly guess from the words and deeds of Jesus Christ that there was anything 'funny' about being a woman.[1]

Jesus' public ministry was extraordinary. He treated men and women with equal respect and dignity. He nurtured and cherished relationships with men and women and urged them to follow Him and to fulfil God's calling upon their lives. Here, then, is complementarianism demonstrated by the Master of its design. He refused

---

1   Dorothy L. Sayers, *Are Women Human?* (Eerdmanns, 1971), p. 68.

to be bound by man-made rules and traditions, and criticized the religious establishment for placing heavy burdens on the people. He showed compassion to those who were the least valued and most vulnerable members of society – children, widows, social outcasts and the poor – but refused to gloss over their sin, for they too needed to repent and believe the good news. He taught people from the Old Testament like they had never heard before and demonstrated His authority over the wind and the sea, over every kind of sickness and disease, over the evil spirits stirred up by His preaching and even over death.

Jesus' attitude towards men
In His encounters with men Jesus demonstrated authority and leadership that many found irresistible...

> As Jesus walked beside the Sea of Galilee, he saw Simon and his brother Andrew casting a net into the lake, for they were fishermen. 'Come, follow me,' Jesus said, 'and I will make you fishers of men.' At once they left their nets and followed him.
>
> When he had gone a little farther, he saw James son of Zebedee and his brother John in a boat, preparing their nets. Without delay he called them, and they left their father Zebedee in the boat with the hired men and followed him. (Mark 1:16-20)

He commended men for their faith in Him...

> Jesus was not far from the house when the centurion sent friends to say to him: 'Lord, don't trouble yourself, for I do not deserve to have you come under my roof. That is why I did not even consider myself worthy to come to you. But say the word, and my servant will be healed. For I myself

am a man under authority, with soldiers under me. I tell this one, "Go," and he goes; and that one, "Come," and he comes. I say to my servant, "Do this," and he does it.'

When Jesus heard this, he was amazed at him, and turning to the crowd following him, he said, 'I tell you, I have not found such great faith even in Israel.' Then the men who had been sent returned to the house and found the servant well. (Luke 7:6-10)

But He was stern in His rebuking of them when needed…

'Woe to you, teachers of the law and Pharisees, you hypocrites! You clean the outside of the cup and dish, but inside they are full of greed and self-indulgence.' (Matt. 23:25)

But when Jesus turned and looked at his disciples, he rebuked Peter. 'Get behind me, Satan!' he said. 'You do not have in mind the things of God, but the things of men.' (Mark 8:33)

Jesus warned them about lusting after women and challenged His disciples to discipline their thoughts and actions in this regard. The penalty for not doing so would be very severe…

'You have heard that it was said, "Do not commit adultery." But I tell you that anyone who looks at a woman lustfully has already committed adultery with her in his heart. If your right eye causes you to sin, gouge it out and throw it away. It is better for you to lose one part of your body than for your whole body to be thrown into hell. And if your right hand causes you to sin, cut it off and throw it away. It is better for you to lose one part of your body than for your whole body to go into hell'. (Matt. 5:27-30)

JESUS' ATTITUDE TOWARDS WOMEN

But if Jesus' attitude towards men was, at times, irresistible, His attitude towards women was even more remarkable. Contrary to Jewish and Roman practices, Jesus honoured women and spoke to them in public...

> On a Sabbath Jesus was teaching in one of the synagogues, and a woman was there who had been crippled by a spirit for eighteen years. She was bent over and could not straighten up at all. When Jesus saw her, he called her forward and said to her, 'Woman, you are set free from your infirmity.' Then he put his hands on her, and immediately she straightened up and praised God. (Luke 13:10-13)

> The woman said, 'I know that Messiah' (called Christ) 'is coming. When he comes, he will explain everything to us.' Then Jesus declared, 'I who speak to you am he.'

> Just then Jesus' disciples returned and were surprised to find him talking with a woman. But no one asked, 'What do you want?' or 'Why are you talking with her?' (John 4:25-27)

Jesus demonstrated His respect and high regard for women in the way He addressed them. He spoke to them in a thoughtful, caring manner and often called them 'daughter'...

> But Jesus kept looking around to see who had touched him. Then the woman, knowing what had happened to her, came and fell at his feet and, trembling with fear, told him the whole truth. He said to her, 'Daughter, your faith has healed you. Go in peace and be freed from your suffering.' (Mark 5:32-34)

> 'Martha, Martha,' the Lord answered, 'you are worried and upset about many things, but only one thing is needed.

Mary has chosen what is better, and it will not be taken away from her.' (Luke 10:41-42)

He understood their vulnerability and alleviated their physical and emotional suffering…

As soon as they left the synagogue, they went with James and John to the home of Simon and Andrew. Simon's mother-in-law was in bed with a fever, and they told Jesus about her. So he went to her, took her hand and helped her up. The fever left her and she began to wait on them. (Mark 1:29-31)

As he approached the town gate, a dead person was being carried out – the only son of his mother, and she was a widow. And a large crowd from the town was with her. When the Lord saw her, his heart went out to her and he said, 'Don't cry.' Then he went up and touched the coffin, and those carrying it stood still. He said, 'Young man, I say to you, get up!' The dead man sat up and began to talk, and Jesus gave him back to his mother. (Luke 7:12-15)

Near the cross of Jesus stood his mother, his mother's sister, Mary the wife of Clopas, and Mary Magdalene. When Jesus saw his mother there, and the disciple whom he loved standing nearby, he said to his mother, 'Dear woman, here is your son,' and to the disciple, 'Here is your mother.' From that time on, this disciple took her into his home. (John 19:25-27)

Jesus didn't gloss over sin in their lives and held women personally responsible for it. But when He confronted them, He did so without condemnation…

The woman said to him, 'Sir, give me this water so that I won't get thirsty and have to keep coming here to draw water.' He told her, 'Go, call your husband and come back.'

'I have no husband,' she replied. Jesus said to her, 'You are right when you say you have no husband. The fact is, you have had five husbands, and the man you now have is not your husband. What you have just said is quite true.' (John 4:15-18)

Jesus straightened up and asked her, 'Woman, where are they? Has no one condemned you?'

'No one, sir,' she said. 'Then neither do I condemn you,' Jesus declared. 'Go now and leave your life of sin.' (John 8:10-11)[2]

And He pronounced forgiveness on those who repented of their sin...

Then Jesus turned toward the woman and said to Simon, 'Do you see this woman? I came into your house. You did not give me any water for my feet, but she wet my feet with her tears and wiped them with her hair. You did not give me a kiss, but this woman, from the time I entered, has not stopped kissing my feet. You did not put oil on my head, but she has poured perfume on my feet. Therefore, I tell you, her many sins have been forgiven – for she loved much. But he who has been forgiven little loves little.' Then Jesus said to her, 'Your sins are forgiven.'

The other guests began to say among themselves, 'Who is this who even forgives sins?' Jesus said to the woman, 'Your faith has saved you; go in peace.' (Luke 7:44-50)

Contrary to accepted rabbinic practices, Jesus regularly used women as illustrations in His teaching...

'The Queen of the South will rise at the judgment with this generation and condemn it; for she came from the ends

---

2   The story of Jesus and the woman caught in adultery is probably authentic even though it did not originally belong to John's gospel and is not found in the earlier and most reliable manuscripts.

of the earth to listen to Solomon's wisdom, and now one greater than Solomon is here.' (Matt. 12:42)

Jesus continued, 'No prophet is accepted in his hometown. I assure you that there were many widows in Israel in Elijah's time, when the sky was shut for three and a half years and there was a severe famine throughout the land. Yet Elijah was not sent to any of them, but to a widow in Zarephath in the region of Sidon.' (Luke 4:24-26)

'Or suppose a woman has ten silver coins and loses one. Does she not light a lamp, sweep the house and search carefully until she finds it? And when she finds it, she calls her friends and neighbours together and says, "Rejoice with me; I have found my lost coin." In the same way, I tell you, there is rejoicing in the presence of the angels of God over one sinner who repents.' (Luke 15:8-10)

He also encouraged and commended the ministry of women...

After this, Jesus travelled about from one town and village to another, proclaiming the good news of the kingdom of God. The Twelve were with him, and also some women who had been cured of evil spirits and diseases: Mary (called Magdalene) from whom seven demons had come out; Joanna the wife of Chuza, the manager of Herod's household; Susanna; and many others. These women were helping to support them out of their own means. (Luke 8:1-3)

While Jesus was in Bethany, reclining at the table in the home of a man known as Simon the Leper, a woman came with an alabaster jar of very expensive perfume, made of pure nard. She broke the jar and poured the perfume on his head. Some of those present were saying indignantly to one another, 'Why this waste of perfume? It could have been sold for more than a year's wages and the money given to the poor.' And they rebuked her harshly.

'Leave her alone,' said Jesus. 'Why are you bothering her? She has done a beautiful thing to me. The poor you will always have with you, and you can help them any time you want. But you will not always have me. She did what she could. She poured perfume on my body beforehand to prepare for my burial. I tell you the truth, wherever the gospel is preached throughout the world, what she has done will also be told, in memory of her.' (Mark 14:3-9)

All four gospels record that it was women who were the first eye-witnesses to the resurrection, either through meeting an angel of the Lord at the empty tomb or seeing Jesus Himself. Both of them told the women to bear witness to what they had seen and heard, despite the fact that the testimony of women was considered to be invalid in Jewish or Roman law at the time…

So the women hurried away from the tomb, afraid yet filled with joy, and ran to tell the disciples [what the angel had told them]. Suddenly Jesus met them. 'Greetings,' he said. They came to him, clasped his feet and worshipped him. Then Jesus said to them, 'Do not be afraid. Go and tell my brothers to go to Galilee; there they will see me.' (Matt. 28:8-10)

When the Sabbath was over, Mary Magdalene, Mary the mother of James, and Salome bought spices so that they might go to anoint Jesus' body. Very early on the first day of the week, just after sunrise, they were on their way to the tomb and they asked each other, 'Who will roll the stone away from the entrance of the tomb?' But when they looked up, they saw that the stone, which was very large, had been rolled away. As they entered the tomb, they saw a young man dressed in a white robe sitting on the right side, and they were alarmed. 'Don't be alarmed,' he said. 'You are looking for Jesus the Nazarene, who was crucified. He has risen! He is not here. See the place where they laid him. But go, tell his disciples and Peter, "He is going ahead of you into Galilee. There you will see him, just as he told you".' (Mark 16:1-7)

On the first day of the week, very early in the morning, the women took the spices they had prepared and went to the tomb. They found the stone rolled away from the tomb, but when they entered, they did not find the body of the Lord Jesus. While they were wondering about this, suddenly two men in clothes that gleamed like lightning stood beside them. In their fright the women bowed down with their faces to the ground, but the men said to them, 'Why do you look for the living among the dead? He is not here; he has risen! Remember how he told you, while he was still with you in Galilee: "The Son of Man must be delivered into the hands of sinful men, be crucified and on the third day be raised again".' Then they remembered his words. When they came back from the tomb, they told all these things to the Eleven and to all the others. It was Mary Magdalene, Joanna, Mary the mother of James, and the others with them who told this to the apostles. (Luke 24:1-10)

Mary stood outside the tomb crying. As she wept, she bent over to look into the tomb and saw two angels in white, seated where Jesus' body had been, one at the head and the other at the foot. They asked her, 'Woman, why are you crying?' 'They have taken my Lord away,' she said, 'and I don't know where they have put him.' At this, she turned around and saw Jesus standing there, but she did not realize that it was Jesus. 'Woman,' he said, 'why are you crying? Who is it you are looking for?' Thinking he was the gardener, she said, 'Sir, if you have carried him away, tell me where you have put him, and I will get him.' Jesus said to her, 'Mary.' She turned toward him and cried out in Aramaic, 'Rabboni!' (which means Teacher). Jesus said, 'Do not hold on to me, for I have not yet returned to the Father. Go instead to my brothers and tell them, "I am returning to my Father and your Father, to my God and your God".' Mary Magdalene went to the disciples with the news: 'I have seen the Lord!' And she told them that he had said these things to her. (John 20:10-18)

Affirming the created order

What's interesting about these accounts is the way all four of them show that the women have a role in testifying to the resurrection and proclaiming the good news of the gospel. But it's also clear from Jesus' earthly ministry that men are to take the lead and have a distinct role, one that women do not share. Jesus upheld the equality of men and women but also re-affirmed that their roles within the nuclear family and the family of God were not the same. In doing so, He re-established God's ordering of relationships and design for men and women and affirmed the equality, diversity and complementarity of men and women.

We see this in a number of different ways...

Marriage

When questioned about divorce, Jesus affirmed the man's initiative in marriage and affirmed that it is a lifelong union between a man and a woman...

Some Pharisees came to Jesus to test him. They asked, 'Is it lawful for a man to divorce his wife for any and every reason?'

'Haven't you read,' Jesus replied, 'that at the beginning the Creator "made them male and female," and said, "For this reason a man will leave his father and mother and be united to his wife, and the two will become one flesh"? So they are no longer two, but one. Therefore what God has joined together, let man not separate.' (Matt. 19:3-6)

Public ministry
He appointed twelve men to be His disciples...

Jesus went up on a mountainside and called to him those he wanted, and they came to him. He appointed twelve – designating them apostles – that they might be with him and that he might send them out to preach and to have authority to drive out demons. These are the twelve he appointed: Simon (to whom he gave the name Peter), James son of Zebedee and his brother John (to them he gave the name Boanerges, which means Sons of Thunder); Andrew, Philip, Bartholomew, Matthew, Thomas, James son of Alphaeus, Thaddaeus, Simon the Zealot and Judas Iscariot, who betrayed him. (Mark 3:13-19)

He commissioned eleven men to be His Apostles...

Then the eleven disciples went to Galilee, to the mountain where Jesus had told them to go. When they saw him, they worshipped him; but some doubted. Then Jesus came to them and said, 'All authority in heaven and on earth has been given to me. Therefore go and make disciples of all nations, baptizing them in the name of the Father and of the Son and of the Holy Spirit, and teaching them to obey everything I have commanded you. And surely I am with you always, to the very end of the age.' (Matt. 28:16-20)

Just before Jesus ascended to heaven, He re-affirmed this Apostolic commission when He called these same eleven men to be His witnesses once they had received power from the Holy Spirit...

> When [the eleven Apostles Jesus had chosen] met together, they asked him, 'Lord, are you at this time going to restore the kingdom to Israel?'
>
> Jesus said to them: 'It is not for you to know the times or dates the Father has set by his own authority. But you will receive power when the Holy Spirit comes on you; and you will be my witnesses in Jerusalem, and in all Judea and Samaria, and to the ends of the earth.'
>
> After he said this, he was taken up before their very eyes, and a cloud hid him from their sight. (Acts 1:6-9)

Jesus valued the ministry of women and went out of His way to show that in following Him they too had an important role to play but their role was not exactly the same as the role of men. Of course, affirming these gender distinctions was not the major focus of His ministry. But as the only flawless man who has ever lived, the one who always obeyed His Father and perfectly represented His Image on earth, we clearly see the pattern of God's design being upheld – both in the way the Lord Jesus went about His ministry and in the way He related to men and women.

CRUSHING THE SERPENT'S HEAD

Despite calling men and women to follow after Him, Jesus knew that only He could go to the cross. He made it clear throughout His ministry that sin was humanity's greatest problem and that only He could deal with it. He was the stronger man who had come to bind up Satan, once and for all, and to plunder his house.[3] Even Satan and the evil spirits knew that Jesus had come to do this…

---

3   See Mark 3:23-27.

Just then a man in their synagogue who was possessed by an evil spirit cried out, 'What do you want with us, Jesus of Nazareth? Have you come to destroy us? I know who you are – the Holy One of God!' (Mark 1:23-24)

When Jesus arrived at the other side in the region of the Gadarenes, two demon-possessed men coming from the tombs met him. They were so violent that no one could pass that way. 'What do you want with us, Son of God?' they shouted. 'Have you come here to torture us before the appointed time?' (Matt. 8:28-29)

Jesus' teaching about the cross

Satan and his agents knew why Jesus had come but the disciples were slow to realise what His real mission was. Mark's Gospel records that Jesus told His disciples three times that they were going to Jerusalem where He would be killed and, after three days, rise again…

Jesus began to teach them that the Son of Man must suffer many things and be rejected by the elders, chief priests and teachers of the law, and that He must be killed and after three days rise again. (Mark 8:31)

Jesus said to them, 'The Son of Man is going to be betrayed into the hands of men. They will kill him, and after three days he will rise.' But they did not understand what he meant and were afraid to ask him about it. (Mark 9:31-32)

'We are going up to Jerusalem,' Jesus said, 'and the Son of Man will be betrayed to the chief priests and teachers of the law. They will condemn him to death and will hand him over to the Gentiles, who will mock him and spit on him, flog him and kill him. Three days later he will rise.' (Mark 10:33-34)

But the disciples just didn't get it. They claimed to be able to follow Jesus wherever He went and did not understand, at least at this stage, why His death was needed to free them from their bondage to sin. The Old Testament prophesied Jesus' coming, and He fulfilled those prophecies throughout His earthly ministry. The disciples certainly believed He was the Messiah, God's chosen King, but they were blind to their need of Him and could not see what He had really come to do.

Full of confidence and consumed by their own self-importance, James and John even asked Jesus to let them sit on either side of Him in glory...

> 'You don't know what you are asking,' Jesus said. 'Can you drink the cup I drink or be baptised with the baptism I am baptised with?'
>
> 'We can,' they answered. (Mark 10:38-39)

The cup Jesus spoke of here is the cup of God's wrath, a picture of His judgment.[4] Jesus' death was a sacrificial death; a sacrifice for sin. The perfect human being, the unblemished Lamb of God, died to take way the sins of the world; God's wrath was poured out on Him, who knew no sin, in order that He might be a sufficient sacrifice for sin and able to take it away.[5]

But there's no indication that the disciples understood any of this at this stage. On the contrary, when the other disciples hear of James and John's request, they are none too pleased...

> When the ten heard about this, they became indignant with James and John. Jesus called them together and said,

---

4   See, for example, Psalm 75:8 and Jeremiah 25:15-16.

5   See, for example, John 1:29, Romans 3:25-26, 1 Thessalonians 1:10, 1 Thessalonians 5:9, 1 Peter 2:22-24, 1 Peter 3:18 and 1 John 2:1-2.

'You know that those who are regarded as rulers of the Gentiles lord it over them, and their high officials exercise authority over them. Not so with you. Instead, whoever wants to become great among you must be your servant, and whoever wants to be first must be slave of all. For even the Son of Man did not come to be served, but to serve, and to give his life as a ransom for many.' (Mark 10:41-45)

Here Jesus tells them something significant about Himself – that He is the Son of Man (an Old Testament title[6] referring to the one to whom God has given all authority and power), who has nevertheless come to be the servant of all. But He also tells them something significant about His death. It will be a substitutionary death, a ransom for many. He dies in their place, bearing the wrath of God Himself so they won't have to. Jesus perfectly represented His Father while on earth. He was the image of the invisible God and as such was the perfect propitiatory sacrifice – the one who was able to turn aside God's wrath and take away our sin. In his masterly book, *The Cross of Christ*, John Stott famously summarises Jesus' atoning death as 'God satisfying Himself by substituting Himself for us.'[7]

Jesus' death on the cross

When Jesus is on the cross, Mark records various clues that, once again, reveal what is really happening…

At the sixth hour darkness came over the whole land until the ninth hour. And at the ninth hour Jesus cried out in a loud voice, 'Eloi, Eloi, lama sabachthani?' – which means, 'My God, my God, why have you forsaken me?'

---

6   See Daniel 7:13-14.

7   John Stott *The Cross of Christ* (IVP, 1986), p. 160.

When some of those standing near heard this, they said, 'Listen, he's calling Elijah.' One man ran, filled a sponge with wine vinegar, put it on a stick, and offered it to Jesus to drink. 'Now leave him alone. Let's see if Elijah comes to take him down,' he said.

With a loud cry, Jesus breathed his last. The curtain of the temple was torn in two from top to bottom. And when the centurion, who stood there in front of Jesus, heard his cry and saw how he died, he said, 'Surely this man was the Son of God!' (Mark 15:33-39)

There are three major clues here as to what Jesus' death is achieving. First of all, darkness covers the earth. In the Old Testament, darkness in the middle of the day was always a sign of God's judgment.[8] Next, there is Jesus' cry, a quote from Psalm 22, that reveals He has been forsaken by God and cut off from His presence – the just penalty for bearing our sin. And lastly, there is the curtain in the temple, which is torn in two from top to bottom, signalling that there is now free access into the presence of God[9] because sin has been dealt with once and for all.

Jesus was a man like no other man. He perfectly represented God's image in the world and remained obedient to His Father's will. He was the second Adam, the second representative, whose perfect life now brings new life to all who trust in Him. In his letter to the Romans, the Apostle Paul compares the consequences of Adam's sin with the consequences of Jesus' obedience...

8　See, for example, Deuteronomy 28:29, Amos 8:9-10 and Jeremiah 15:9.

9　See Hebrews 6:19-20 and Hebrews 10:19-22.

> Consequently, just as the result of one trespass was condemna-
> tion for all men, so also the result of one act of righteousness was
> justification that brings life for all men. For just as through the
> disobedience of the one man (Adam) the many were made sin-
> ners, so also through the obedience of the one man (Jesus) the
> many will be made righteous. (Rom. 5:18-19)

Jesus came to crush Satan's head and free humanity from
the tyranny of sin. His death and resurrection heralded
the dawn of a new age, the culmination of which will
result in all the benefits of Eden being restored. Because
of Christ's sacrifice, the penalty of sin has been dealt
with once and for all, and those who trust in His death
are brought back into relationship with their Creator
and can enjoy the blessings of a restored relationship
with each other. Sin is still present, but it does not have
the same power as it used to.

After Jesus ascended into heaven, He poured out
the Holy Spirit on His people. The Spirit dwells within
the hearts of all those who trust in Jesus' death for the
forgiveness of their sins. He is a deposit, guaranteeing
our future inheritance in glory; He testifies with
our spirits that we are truly God's children, and He
intercedes for us with groans that words cannot express
in accordance with God's will.[10] The Spirit grants gifts
to all God's people, that they might learn to serve one
another, and He produces fruit in their lives, that they
might become more like Jesus.[11]

This means that Christians today have the huge
privilege of living in the age of the Spirit. But with this
privilege there comes great responsibility. In response
to His grace, we are to live lives that reflect the Lord

---

10   See Ephesians 1:13-14, Romans 8:16-17 and Romans 8:26-27.

11   See 1 Corinthians 12:7-11 and Galatians 5:22-25.

Jesus and demonstrate that the Spirit is at work within us – enabling us to live for Him and serve other people. With Satan now overthrown we do not have to live like we used to. We are free to live as God intended. God's design was revealed in creation; it was rejected at the Fall, but it is, now, wonderfully, restored in Christ. But what are the implications of this for marriage and family life? That is the subject of the next chapter.

DISCUSSION QUESTIONS FOR GROUPS/INDIVIDUALS

1. How did Jesus demonstrate that He is not like any other man?

2. How did He show His respect and appreciation for women, in particular?

3. What did His death on the cross achieve?

4. What are the implications of Satan being overthrown?

5. How should we pray in light of these truths?

7

The Implications of God's design for marriage

Pete and Sue were happily married with two teenage girls. They had lived on the outskirts of a large city for over fifteen years and seemed very settled. But their lives were turned upside down when Pete's company took a sudden downturn and he was made redundant. Pete and Sue were still coming to terms with this when, completely out of the blue, Pete was offered a new job in a town two hundred miles away.

Sue was devastated and very reluctant to uproot the family and move away. The girls were settled at school, where they had lots of friends, and they really enjoyed the youth group at church. They were learning to follow the Lord for themselves and, in recent months, had made bold stands for Him at school. Sue, herself, led one of the women's Bible studies at church and felt very attached to the ladies in her group – some of whom she'd known for ten years or more. Her heart ached at the thought of leaving them behind and moving to a new town where she would have no friends.

She talked with Pete and told him why she thought it was not a good time to move the family. What if the girls didn't settle at their new schools? What if they couldn't find a church to go to? Surely a move like this could have a serious impact on their spiritual growth? And if the girls drifted away from the Lord, they would never forgive themselves. But Pete was not unaware of these issues and wanted to entrust them all into the Lord's hands. The job market was not that strong, he needed to work, and the job he was being offered would bring greater security than his previous one. He was of the opinion that they should move and asked Sue to support him in the decision.

To submit or not to submit – is that really the question? Faced with this difficult task, Sue sought the counsel of a trusted friend and asked her what she should do – should she submit to Pete and move the family to this new town or should she put her foot down and refuse to go? She talked with her friend for a couple of hours and gradually started to realise that the issue was far bigger than just whether or not she should submit to her husband. In fact, she wondered if that was really the right question to be asking at all.

Surely the bigger issue was whether or not she could trust the Lord in all this – as Pete was keen to do. She also realised that her attitude was absolutely key. Pete had not just asked her to go along with his decision, but to support him in it. She therefore had a choice. She could decide to go with a negative and bitter attitude, but that wouldn't help Pete much and was bound to be picked up by the children; or she could trust that the Lord was more than able to help them and go with a positive and healthy attitude.

At the end of the day, it wasn't just about whether she would submit to Pete, but whether or not she would submit to the Lord and trust that He would be faithful to His Word. She prayed about it with her friend and then went home to tell Pete that she would support him – slightly fearful but nonetheless trusting that the Lord would be with them as they embarked on this new and rather daunting venture.

Whatever you think of Sue's decision, I think it is fair to say that submission is not a very popular concept today. No doubt, like me, you've heard some of the murmuring that goes on at the end of a wedding service when the bride has promised to love, honour and obey her husband. 'I can't believe she said that! Surely she doesn't really mean it! Her husband will walk all over her! That's so sad, and I thought she was such an intelligent woman!'

But a wife's willingness to submit to her husband is not a sign of weakness, nor is it an open invitation to be used as a doormat. Rightly understood, it is the demonstration of her commitment and trust in a man charged with the responsibility of exercising protective leadership. And when they both play their part it can be quite beautiful. Of course, we move in and out of different types of submissive relationships all the time. As a teenager at school, I had to submit to my teachers but years later, when some of those teachers later became my colleagues, the relationship changed. A senior consultant might exercise leadership over her colleagues in a hospital department, but they are all subject to the speeding restrictions on the roads surrounding the hospital that are imposed by the local authority. A pastor may exercise teaching authority in his church on a Sunday, but he will need to submit to the civil enforcement officer who gives him a parking ticket the following afternoon – even if she's a member of his congregation!

The New Testament clearly teaches that a wife should submit to her husband. This is what being in Christ and living in the age of the Spirit will involve, even if her husband is not a believer...

> Wives, submit to your husbands, as is fitting in the Lord. Husbands, love your wives and do not be harsh with them. (Col. 3:18-19)

> Wives, in the same way be submissive to your husbands so that, if any of them do not believe the word, they may be won over without words by the behaviour of their wives, when they see the purity and reverence of your lives. (1 Pet. 3:1-2)

This teaching about submission in marriage may be rather contentious in the modern era, but when Paul expands on why it is so important, for example in Ephesians 5, we see that a wife's submission to her husband does not make her inferior to her husband. In fact, there is something much more significant going on here. And if you're a single woman reading this and beginning to switch off because you think there is nothing here for you, think again! This passage is central to our understanding of what it means to be a Christian and how we can encourage one another in our walk with the Lord...

> Wives, submit to your husbands as to the Lord. For the husband is the head of the wife as Christ is the head of the church, his body, of which he is the Saviour. Now as the church submits to Christ, so also wives should submit to their husbands in everything.

Husbands, love your wives, just as Christ loved the church and gave himself up for her to make her holy, cleansing her by the washing with water through the word, and to present her to himself as a radiant church, without stain or wrinkle or any other blemish, but holy and blameless. In this same way, husbands ought to love their wives as their own bodies. He who loves his wife loves himself. After all, no one ever hated his own body, but he feeds and cares for it, just as Christ does the church – for we are members of his body. 'For this reason a man will leave his father and mother and be united to his wife, and the two will become one flesh.' This is a profound mystery – but I am talking about Christ and the church. However, each one of you also must love his wife as he loves himself, and the wife must respect her husband. (Eph. 5:22-33)

Paul writes to the Ephesian church, which he founded, to encourage them to live a life worthy of their calling. In the first half of the letter he has reminded them of the many blessings they have as Christians – they are chosen, adopted, redeemed and included in Christ; they are marked and sealed by the promised Holy Spirit, who is a deposit guaranteeing their future inheritance; they were dead in their sins and under God's wrath but, because of His mercy and love, they are now saved by His grace, through faith in Christ. As Gentiles, they were once alienated from God and far from Him, but now, through the blood of Christ, they have been brought near and are fellow-citizens with all God's people and are members of His household.

The second half of the letter focuses on the practical outworking of these blessings. God's design for humanity, for both men and women, was revealed in creation and then ruined at the Fall, but it is now wonderfully restored in Christ. As a result, these Ephesian Christians need to live lives that are worthy of the Lord, which means preserving the unity they have in Christ. This will, inevitably, have an impact on the way they live – not just at church, where they are to use the gifts God has given them to build up the body of Christ, but also at home, in their family life.

In this part of chapter five, Paul shows what sort of impact being included in Christ should have on their marriages but, interestingly, it's not just those who are married who he has in mind here, as we shall see. He addresses wives and husbands separately and in doing so seeks to affirm the foundational principles of Genesis 1 and 2 – that men and women are equal in their dignity, status and worth but have different roles in marriage. He turns his attention to the wives, first of all...

Humble submission

Being included in Christ and marked by the Spirit means wives need to show humble submission...

> Wives, submit to your husbands as to the Lord. For the husband is head of the wife as Christ is head of the church, his body, of which he is the Saviour. Now as the church submits to Christ, so also wives should submit to their husbands in everything. (Eph. 5:22-24)

Paul's instruction here is often misunderstood, so it's worth being clear about what he is and isn't saying. Note that a wife is to submit to her husband and *not* to every man she knows. As a child, she submitted to her parents, but once she enters into a covenant relationship with her husband, she is to submit to him. The command to honour her parents still stands, but she does not have to submit to them. Marriage changes the nature of all our relationships and a wife's priority, after the Lord, is to her husband.

Note too, that she is to submit to her husband in *everything* – not just when it's easy to submit to him and she wants to, but also when it's hard and she doesn't. It is to be a voluntary submission, one that she chooses to give, and not demanded of her by her husband. And before we think that the Lord is asking wives to do something here that He never had to do Himself, it's worth remembering that in the Garden of Gethsemane Jesus was the *perfect* model of humble submission...

> Going a little farther, Jesus fell to the ground and prayed that if possible the hour might pass from him. 'Abba, Father,' he said, 'everything is possible for you. Take this cup from me. Yet not what I will, but what you will.' (Mark 14:35-36)

> He withdrew about a stone's throw beyond them, knelt down and prayed, 'Father, if you are willing, take this cup from me; yet not my will, but yours be done.' An angel from heaven appeared to him and strengthened him. And being in anguish, he prayed more earnestly, and his sweat was like drops of blood falling to the ground. (Luke 22:41-44)

Similarly, Paul writes about the Lord Jesus in his letter to the Philippians...

> [Jesus], being in very nature God,
> > did not consider equality with God something to be grasped,
> but made himself nothing,
> > taking the very nature of a servant,
> > being made in human likeness.
> And being found in appearance as a man,
> > he humbled himself and became obedient to death -
> > even death on a cross! (Phil. 2:6-8)

Jesus humbly submitted to His Father's will in everything, and wives too are to submit to their husbands in everything. And, as we saw in chapter 2, this submission does not mean that Jesus is passive or inferior to His Father any more than it means a wife is passive or inferior to her husband. The difference between a wife and her husband is a functional one and is designed to maintain good order.

I take it that this means a wife should submit to her husband even when she doesn't agree with him and that she shouldn't take the 'I-told-you-so' attitude when a decision he makes turns out to be the wrong one. But I also understand that this won't be easy to do, as our natural tendency is to plead our case and insist on our rights – something that Jesus voluntarily surrendered. So, we should expect the practice of submission to be difficult and, at times, quite painful, but the Lord is clear on this. Christian wives who love the Lord and want to live for Him need to submit to their husbands in everything and, if they don't, they will have to suffer the consequences.

This reminds me of another couple, who faced a similar predicament to Pete and Sue, but things turned out very differently for them. Gavin and Jo lived in a large town and had three children under ten. Gavin was offered a promotion at work, but taking it would mean relocating to the office in London, three hundred miles away. Jo didn't want to uproot the family and move away. The children were settled at school, they had good networks of friends, and they all enjoyed being part of the church Sunday school.

The big difference between the two families was Jo's attitude in dealing with the proposed move. She behaved very differently to Sue. She refused to move and told her friends how unfair it was of her husband to consider taking the family so far away. For quite a while it was all she ever talked about. In the end she wore her husband down and he let the promotion go – just to stop her nagging. He continued working at the same level and all seemed to be well.

It was some years later that Jo told me her insistence they stayed had had a devastating impact on their marriage. Over a period of some months, Gavin withdrew from making any decisions at all, so she had to take on more and more leadership in the marriage. At first, she quite enjoyed this, but in the end it meant she became the dominant parent in the family and she had to raise the children on her own. Gavin said he felt useless in the marriage and foolish in the eyes of his friends – who thought he'd been weak in giving in to Jo's nagging. It wasn't long before he started drifting spiritually and stopped going to church.

Two wives, facing similar challenges, with two very different outcomes – because the ways they dealt with them were so different. One trusted that submitting to her husband was the right thing to do, but the other refused to respect his leadership – and effectively emasculated him in the process. But why does God place what seems to be such a heavy burden on women in marriage? Why is submission to their husbands so important? The answer comes a little further on in the passage...

> For the husband is the head of the wife as Christ is the head of the church, his body, of which he is the Saviour. (Eph. 5:23)

It's because of what the marriage signifies. Marriage is a picture, a visual aid if you like, of another more significant relationship – that of Christ and the church. The husband is head of the wife just as Christ is head of the church. As the church submits to Christ in everything, so wives are to submit to their husbands in everything. This means that a wife's submission to her husband is ultimately part of her submission to Christ. This means that when a wife refuses to submit to her husband, she is ultimately refusing to submit to the Lord.

But what about husbands, what does being in Christ mean for them? Paul says they must show…

SACRIFICIAL LOVE

Being in Christ and marked by the Spirit means husbands need to show sacrificial love…

> Husbands, love your wives, just as Christ loved the church and gave himself up for her to make her holy, cleansing her by the washing with water through the word, and to present her to himself as a radiant church, without stain or wrinkle or any other blemish, but holy and blameless. In this same way, husbands ought to love their wives as their own bodies. He who loves his wife loves himself. After all, no one ever hated his own body, but he feeds and cares for it, just as Christ does the church. (Eph. 5:25-29)

If we think humble submission is a tall order for wives, the command here for husbands is no less demanding. In fact, the standard required of them may be even harder. They are to love their wives as Christ loved the church, which means loving them sacrificially, even to the point of giving themselves up for them. As head of the family they are to nurture, protect, and care for their wives – even if it means dying to protect them from harm. And, once again, it is the Lord Jesus Himself who provides the perfect model for them to follow.

'I am the good shepherd. The good shepherd lays down his life for the sheep.' (John 10:11)

'The reason my Father loves me is that I lay down my life. No one takes it from me, but I lay it down of my own accord.' (John 10:17-18)

'Greater love has no one than this that he lay down his life for his friends.' (John 15:13)

But, once again, we need to be clear about what Paul is and isn't saying. He isn't saying that a husband is to die for his wife in exactly the same way as Christ died for the church. No – only the Lord is able to die for her sins and make her holy and blameless in God's sight. But her husband is to nurture and protect her, even if it means making the ultimate sacrifice for her.

I guess this may explain why husbands instinctively shield their wives from danger or harm; why the lifeboats on the Titanic were filled, first of all, with women and children. It seems as though it may be part of the God-given male psyche that when trouble comes, husbands jump in front of their wives. You certainly don't hear of many wives jumping in front of their husbands! In fact, women are far more likely to shield their children; but it's the husband who will instinctively jump in front of his wife to save her. This is part of his leadership role – even if it means dying in the process.

Of course, people are very fearful of the abuse of leadership that can sometimes happen in marriage but that is not what is being condoned here. A man's leadership of his wife is not a recipe for tyranny, nor is she expected to be a doormat. On the contrary, the wife needs to help her husband by telling him what she thinks, and then leaving him to make an informed decision. The husband, in turn, needs to realise that loving his wife means taking account of her feelings, her intuitions and her experiential knowledge as a woman and maybe also as a mother. It is certainly true that where I have seen a husband's leadership of his wife work well it has always involved him listening to his wife and taking her point of view into account. This doesn't mean that a husband should necessarily let his wife's thinking replace his own but loving leadership will involve serious consideration of her point of view.

But that's not all. Paul reminds them that when a husband and wife marry, they are united together and become one flesh. And the husband is to love his wife as he loves his own body. This doesn't just mean caring for her in a physical sense, because he is also given the responsibility of making sure that they remain in Christ. He is to be the spiritual head of the family and ensure that the Word of God continues to feed, wash and cleanse them, so they are holy and blameless before the Lord when He comes.

I'm not someone who cries easily at weddings, but I do remember tears welling up at one particular reception. David had just married Elizabeth and was giving the customary bridegroom's speech. He'd already toasted the bridesmaids but, before sitting down, he turned to address his wife of a couple of hours. He said something like this: 'My darling Elizabeth, I love you more than you will ever know, but you must remember that there is someone else in our marriage who is more important than me. He is the real bridegroom and He's given me the task of preparing you for Him. To help me do that you must love Him more than me and remember that, for now, I am just the very poor stand-in.'

Now there's a man who has the right perspective on his marriage and knows that it is not an end in itself but rather a means to a greater end! In fact, the whole of our earthly lives are just the preamble, the preparation for something far, far greater – but more on that in chapter ten.

Husbands are to love their wives, as Christ loved the church. It is a high standard to attain and needs to be shown voluntarily. The wife can't demand to be loved like this, just as her husband can't demand that she submits to him. Ultimately, they are both accountable to Christ and must both submit to *His* commands – the husband submits to Christ by sacrificially loving his wife and the wife submits to Christ by voluntarily submitting to her husband.

Objections

Some people object to all this on the grounds that, surely, the New Testament teaches that there should be mutual submission in marriage? A wife will sometimes submit to her husband and a husband will sometimes submit to his wife. Those who hold this view try to argue it from Ephesians 5 where Paul says...

Submit to one another out of reverence for Christ. (Eph. 5:21)

The trouble with this interpretation is that we then have to say that Paul was arguing for mutual submission in the family, with parents submitting to their children (Eph. 6:1-4) and in the wider community, with masters submitting to their slaves (Eph. 6:5-9) – both of which are unworkable. Ephesians 5:21 is far more likely to be introducing the idea of submission out of reverence to Christ which is then illustrated in three ways – wives to husbands, children to parents, and slaves to masters. It is also more likely to be defining what being filled with the Spirit looks like – and serves as just one example, with others being listed in Ephesians 5:18-20. The ESV translation is, perhaps, a little more helpful here than the NIV…

> Do not get drunk with wine, for that is debauchery, but be filled with the Spirit, addressing one another in psalms and hymns and spiritual songs, singing and making melody to the Lord with your heart, giving thanks always and for everything to God the Father in the name of our Lord Jesus Christ, submitting to one another out of reverence for Christ. (Eph. 5:18-21, esv)

Of course, this doesn't mean that husbands won't sometimes do what their wives want – but when they do, they are not submitting to them; they are exercising loving leadership. They are equal partners in the marriage and, as I've indicated already, the wife must tell her husband what she thinks. Even the most noble of men cannot read a woman's mind! But, because he is the head of the family and given the task of leading, she must leave the decision to him, and submit to it when it is made. This is how good order in marriage is to be achieved and maintained, reflecting once again the unity and order within the Trinity.

Reversing the effects of the Fall

But, in the goodness of the Lord, I wonder if there is something else going on here? We know that the battle of the sexes came as a punishment for sin in Genesis 3 and has been raging in every generation since then. A wife's natural, fallen tendency is to control and manipulate her husband; and a husband's natural, fallen tendency is to abdicate his leadership or dominate his wife abusively.

But here, in Ephesians 5, there are two commands that will actually counteract these sinful tendencies. A naturally controlling and manipulative wife must learn to submit to her husband and a naturally abusive or abdicating husband must learn to love his wife. If they do this then the created order of Genesis 2 is restored to a degree, and they can begin to enjoy something of the open, honest, and harmonious relationship that marriage was always intended to be.

Wayne Grudem says something similar when he argues that in marriage the common errors of passivity and aggression are avoided if we hold to the Biblical ideal. The following table seeks to illustrate his point...[1]

	Error of passivity	Biblical Ideal	Error of aggression
Husband	Wimp (leadership abdicated)	Sacrificial love	Tyrant (partnership abused)
Wife	Doormat (partnership destroyed)	Voluntary submission	Usurper (leadership challenged)

What's interesting here is how the error of aggression in one partner can lead to the error of passivity in the other. A tyrannical husband, who abuses his wife, will inevitably have an influence on his wife – who may become a doormat as the path of least resistance. A usurping wife, who manipulates and controls her husband, will inevitably have an influence on her husband – who may turn into a wimp; anything for an easy life. Those who hold to the Biblical ideal should have a more positive impact on their marriages.

1　Wayne Grudem, 'Gender Distinctives' (Council for Biblical Manhood and Womanhood Conference, Oxford, June 2002).

A godly husband, who loves his wife sacrificially, will avoid being a wimp or a tyrant. A godly wife, who voluntarily submits to her husband, will avoid being a doormat or a usurper.

When viewed in this light, these commands are not heavy burdens placed upon us by an unreasonable God but helpful correctives that enable us to enjoy something of the blessing of marriage as He intended. Now, let's be honest, there is no such thing as a perfect marriage, not in this life anyway, but Christians who trust the Lord and submit to His Word on this will find that their marriages are transformed. Not sure if you believe me? Well, there's only one way to find out!

THE REAL MARRIAGE – THAT OF CHRIST AND THE CHURCH

But before we get too preoccupied with the restoration of our earthly marriages, we must be careful not to ignore what this passage says about the marriage between Christ and the church...

> No one ever hated his own body, but he feeds and cares for it, just as Christ does the church – for we are members of his body. 'For this reason a man will leave his father and mother and be united to his wife and the two will become one flesh.' This is a profound mystery – but I am talking about Christ and the church. However, each one of you also must love his wife as he loves himself, and the wife must respect her husband. (Eph. 5:29-33)

Paul teaches the Ephesian Christians about earthly marriage in order that they might understand something far more profound. A marriage between a man and a woman may be the closest human relationship of all, but it is not the most important relationship a human can have. The reason for this is because earthly marriage is temporary and just for this life. If you are married, your husband won't be your husband in heaven – he will be your brother. In the grand scheme of things, earthly marriage isn't the most significant relationship because it doesn't last forever. Now don't get me wrong, marriage is a good gift from the Lord and comes with many blessings in this life, but it is also a pointer to a much more significant relationship – that of the marriage between Christ and His church, which lasts for all eternity.

It is the Lord Jesus Christ who is the *real* husband, who loves His bride and gave Himself up for her to save her. He is the one who nurtures and protects her, who cleanses her and makes her holy; He washes her through His Word and makes sure that she is without any stain, wrinkle or blemish. He is the one who makes her radiant and blameless and then presents her to Himself for all eternity.

Christian marriage is a small picture of this heavenly marriage and an essential visual aid for *all* Christians. So when I, a single woman, see a Christian wife humbly submitting to her husband as head of the family, it is a reminder to me that I need to submit to Christ, the *real* husband, who is head of the church. Similarly, when I see a Christian husband loving his wife sacrificially, it is a reminder to me of Christ's sacrificial love for His bride, the church.

These visible demonstrations of sacrificial love and humble submission are an important reminder of what the Lord has done for us, what our response should be, and where we are ultimately heading. This means that Christian marriage is never an end in itself, nor is it just for the two who are married to each other. It is an important visual aid for the whole community and a means to understanding something far more significant. A Christian family is a microcosm of the universal church family and, as such, should show us what it means to live with Jesus as our head. Men and women, whether young or old, rich or poor, married or single, are to live in humble submission to Him – and those who are married have a distinctive way of modelling that for the whole community.

What submission to the Lord means in practice will vary according to our gender, our age and our stage of life. What is clear is that being in Christ brings different responsibilities for different people, but the end point is the same for all of us – with the bride of Christ finally presented to the greatest bridegroom of them all. So however good a Christian marriage may be, it can never be as good as the *real* marriage that is to come.

FOUNDATIONAL PRINCIPLES RESTORED

Being in Christ means that the foundational principles revealed in creation can be restored to some degree to their pre-Fall condition.

[1] Supremacy ➜ Equality

Instead of a battle for supremacy, there is a return to equality – we are all one in Christ; we are equal in salvation, equally marked by the Spirit and heirs together of the life that is to come...

> And you also were included in Christ when you heard the word of truth, the gospel of your salvation. Having believed, you were marked in him with a seal, the promised Holy Spirit, who is a deposit guaranteeing our inheritance until the redemption of those who are God's possession – to the praise of his glory. (Eph. 1:13-14)

> For it is by grace you have been saved, through faith – and
> this not from yourselves, it is the gift of God – not by works,
> so that no one can boast. (Eph. 2:8-9)

[2] Uniformity ➔ Diversity

Instead of a quest for uniformity, there is a return to
the glorious diversity that God intended for men and
women – with men showing sacrificial love as they lead
their wives and women showing humble submission
as they help their husbands…

> Wives, submit to your husbands as to the Lord. For the
> husband is the head of the wife as Christ is the head of the
> church, his body, of which he is the Saviour. Now as the
> church submits to Christ, so also wives should submit to
> their husbands in everything.

> Husbands, love your wives, just as Christ loved the church
> and gave himself up for her, cleansing her by the washing
> with water through the word, and to present her to himself
> as a radiant church, without stain or wrinkle or any other
> blemish, but holy and blameless. (Eph. 5:22-27)

[3] Conflict ➔ Complementarity

And instead of conflict, there is a return to complementarity, as men and women demonstrate their dependence on each other in fulfilling their God-given roles.
Only when men and women acknowledge their equality in status and yet their diversity in role can they bring
unity and completeness to one another…

> I urge you to live a life worthy of the calling you have
> received. Be completely humble and gentle; be patient,
> bearing with one another in love. Make every effort to keep
> the unity of the Spirit through the bond of peace. There is

one body and one Spirit – just as you were called to one hope
when you were called – one Lord, one faith, one baptism;
one God and Father of all, who is over all and through all
and in all. (Eph. 4:1-6)

So, what does this mean *specifically* for Christian women,
today?

For women who are married

For those who are married, it means that submission to
your husband is key and needs to be given voluntarily
– just as Christ willingly surrendered to His Father's
will and trusted that He knew what He was asking and
would be faithful to His Word.

The Apostle Peter writes in his first letter that 'When
they hurled their insults at him, Jesus did not retaliate;
when he suffered he made no threats. Instead he entrusted
himself to him who judges justly' – and was then gloriously
vindicated at the resurrection. Peter goes on to say in the
very next section that, 'Wives, in the same way, (in the
same way as Jesus), be submissive to your husbands so
that, if any of them do not believe, they may be won over
by the behaviour of their wives' (1 Pet. 3:1-2).

This may sound shocking, but Peter is quite clear –
even if your husband is not a believer, you are still to
submit to him – because this is what the Lord wants you
to do. Some women may have Christian husbands who
do not seem to sacrificially love them, as they should.
But that is no excuse. We will all individually stand
before the Lord and give Him an account of how we
have lived. A godly wife will submit to her husband,
even if he isn't behaving as the Lord wants him to.

Peter says later in the same passage that wives
should do what is right and not give in to fear. It will take

enormous courage to live like this, but women who do will bring honour to the Lord and, what's more, they will encourage other Christians to submit to Him, as they should.

And this is where you can be a real help to those of us who are single. You know, sometimes it's really hard when you hedge us in with questions about our love lives, and encourage us to always be on the look-out for a man. You do not know if the Lord will give us a husband! Instead, it would help us much more if you were able to encourage us to trust the Lord in this area of our lives and submit to His will. And the best way that you can do this is by your own humble submission to His Word.

But what about those of us who are single?

For women who are 'not yet' married
We need to get our thinking straight on this issue. Marriage is a precious gift from the Lord, but not all of us will experience it in this life. We will need to learn to live with those unfulfilled longings and realise that even the best husband in the world wouldn't satisfy them fully. The Lord knows what is best for us and wants us to trust Him. So singleness is not a curse to be avoided at all costs! It brings unique opportunities that our married friends don't have in quite the same way.

But that doesn't mean we don't have any responsibilities towards them. I take it that we should encourage our married friends to submit to their husbands, and to learn to do this willingly and with a good attitude. Then, maybe, we will learn to willingly submit to the Lord ourselves – even if it means we never marry this side of eternity.

GOD'S DESIGN FOR WOMEN – RESTORED IN CHRIST
Whatever our current situation, God's design for women has been wonderfully restored – in Christ. Our

relationship with God has been restored, and we are no longer banished from His presence. We have been washed by His Word and made holy.

In the present, we do not have to live as we used to – our controlling and manipulative tendencies can be changed as we submit ourselves to His will, and to our husbands, if we are married. But married or single, we are free to live a life worthy of the Lord – enjoying the diversity of roles that He delights in and playing our part in the complementarity of men and women in the family.

But the family is not the only arena where our diversity of roles needs to be played out for the glory of God and the benefit of others. The New Testament is quite clear that men and women also have different roles to play in the life of the local church. This is what we will be looking at in the next chapter.

Discussion questions for groups/individuals

1. Why do women naturally find the notion of submitting to their husbands so repugnant?

2. Why do men naturally shrink from the responsibility of loving their wives sacrificially?

3. How is the Lord Jesus a model of both humble submission and sacrificial love?

4. How will our natural, sinful tendencies be counteracted by these commands?

5. How does this passage about marriage encourage those who are single?

8

The Implications
of God's design for the church

Emily has been working on the staff team of a local
church for five years. Initially, her responsibilities were
in children's work but, more recently, the arrival of two
apprentices to help in the running of the Sunday school
has given her opportunities to branch out and do some
ministry among the women in the congregation. She
studies the Bible one-to-one with three different women
– one who is a new Christian, one who is interested
in Christianity but not yet believing, and still another
whom she hopes might study the Bible one-to-one with
other women in the future. She also leads a women's
Bible study on a Thursday morning and, from time
to time, speaks at a women's brunch on a Saturday
morning. She is clearly gifted at teaching the Bible, and
many of the women in the church have appreciated her
clear and challenging talks, which have been helpfully
applied to them as women.

Emily came to talk to me some months ago because
she was feeling pressured by some people in the

congregation who think she ought to go to theological
college and get ordained. They argue that someone
with her kind of teaching gifts should be freed up to
teach the whole church and ordination would open
the door to new and exciting opportunities. They also
say it would give her the wider recognition that her
gifts deserve. Her role, at present, is to work among
the women and children, but some of the congregation
think that is too narrow a role and want her to have
a bigger platform so that the wider church might
benefit from her gifts.

When I met with her, Emily said that it was ironic
that people thought she should pursue even more
ministry opportunities when she, herself, was thinking
that she couldn't really keep up with the ministry she
was doing. She told me she wasn't sleeping very well,
she often felt overwhelmed by the responsibilities she
had; she found it hard to maintain the pace of ministry
and didn't seem to be able to see as many people as
her male colleagues. This meant that she felt rather
lightweight on the team and wondered if she was really
cut out for Bible teaching ministry at all.

Emily's predicament is, sadly, not that uncommon
for women in full-time Bible teaching ministry and
illustrates some of the ways that the homogenisation of
our culture has impacted the life of the local church. Not
only are women being pushed into inappropriate roles
for inappropriate reasons, but the way they are expected
to exercise them is often very masculine. Of course,
some people would argue that the homogenisation of
our culture is a good thing. If you treat men and women
the same, you don't risk offending anyone, or limiting
anyone, or hindering anyone. But, as one American
pastor puts it...

What if God created men and women differently? What if it's not a question of limitations but a matter of distinct divine purposes for different parts of the body? I guess you could say that the eye is limited because it cannot hear. Or that the ear is limited because it cannot see. But that would be missing the point, wouldn't it? The egalitarianism of Western culture, for all its good purposes, leads to the homogenisation of men and women, to unisex clothes, colognes, roles, and lifestyles. The lovely and distinct colour palettes of men and women then mush together into a grey-brown muck.[1]

The aim of this chapter is to show that God's design for men and women has important implications for the life of the local church. Where these are ignored there is confusion and disorder – which not only dishonours the name of the Lord, but also reduces the effectiveness of the church's ministry. Jesus said that it would be by our love for one another that all people would know that we are His disciples.[2] Where that love has been replaced by competitiveness or conflict, the church is ridiculed and open to the charge of hypocrisy.

EQUAL IN SALVATION

The equality of men and women in salvation is clearly upheld in the New Testament. We are equally redeemed, equally included into Christ, and equally marked out by the Holy Spirit. There is no suggestion anywhere in the Bible that redeemed men are in any way more important or more precious to God than redeemed women...

---

1   Jonathan Leeman, 'Understanding and honoring distinctness' (9 Marks eJournal, July/Aug 2010, Volume 7, Issue 3).

2   See John 13:35.

For God so loved the world that he gave his one and only
Son, that whoever believes in him shall not perish but have
eternal life. (John 3:16)

For he (the Father) has rescued us from the dominion of
darkness and brought us into the kingdom of the Son he
loves, in whom we have redemption, the forgiveness of
sins. (Col. 1:13-14)

And you also were included in Christ when you heard
the word of truth, the gospel of your salvation. Having
believed, you were marked in him with a seal, the promised
Holy Spirit, who is a deposit guaranteeing our inheritance
until the redemption of those who are God's possession – to
the praise of his glory. (Eph. 1:13-14)

As well as being marked by the Spirit, men and women
receive gifts from the Spirit and are expected to use
them for the benefit of others...

Now to each one the manifestation of the Spirit is given for
the common good. (1 Cor. 12:7)

Each one should use whatever gift he has received to serve
others, faithfully administering God's grace in its various
forms. If anyone speaks, he should do it as one speaking the
very words of God. If anyone serves, he should do it with
the strength God provides, so that in all things God may be
praised through Jesus Christ. (1 Pet. 4:10-11)

These last two passages cause some people to think
that teaching gifts should be exercised in similar
contexts and that it doesn't really matter who has
them – it could be a man, it could be a woman. But
while the New Testament affirms that some women
as well as some men will have teaching gifts, the way
those teaching gifts are to be exercised will be slightly

different, because God's purposes for men and women within the body of Christ are determined by the order of their creation.

That said, there are some occasions in Scripture where both men and women are expected to teach one another informally...

> Speak to one another with psalms, hymns and spiritual songs. Sing and make music in your heart to the Lord, always giving thanks to God the Father for everything, in the name of our Lord Jesus Christ. (Eph. 5:19-20)

> Let the word of Christ dwell in you richly as you teach and admonish one another with all wisdom, and as you sing psalms, hymns and spiritual songs with gratitude in your hearts to God. (Col. 3:16)

There is no suggestion in either letter that Paul is only writing to men at this point. Nevertheless, there are clearly some other, more formal contexts where it is inappropriate for women to teach men or to exercise authority over them. While men and women may have functional differences in the body of the church, that neither makes one superior to the other nor one less important than the other. As brothers and sisters in Christ, we belong to each other and need each other. The analogy of the body works very well here...

> Now the body is not made up of one part but of many. If the foot should say, 'Because I am not a hand, I do not belong to the body,' it would not for that reason cease to be part of the body. And if the ear should say, 'Because I am not an eye, I do not belong to the body,' it would not for that reason cease to be part of the body. If the whole body were an eye, where would the sense of hearing be? If the whole body were an ear, where would the sense of smell be? But God

has arranged the parts in the body, every one of them, just as he wanted them to be. If they were all one part, where would the body be? As it is, there are many parts, but one body. The eye cannot say to the hand, 'I don't need you!' And the head cannot say to the feet, 'I don't need you!' (1 Cor. 12:14-21)

So it is with men and women. God has given us different roles in the life of the local church, but that does not mean we don't belong to each other. Neither does it mean we don't need each other. The pastor cannot say to the children in his congregation, 'Because you're not pastors, I don't need you!' Neither can the Sunday school teacher say, 'Because I'm not the pastor, I'm not really needed here!' God delights in both the unity and diversity of His church.

DIFFERENT IN FUNCTION

We have already seen that Jesus appointed men (and not women) to be His twelve disciples and then after His resurrection, to be His eleven apostles. The apostles themselves understood the significance of this and when it came to appointing a replacement for Judas Iscariot (who betrayed Jesus and later hanged himself), they chose a man and not a woman.

Peter made it clear on what basis the candidate was to be a suitable replacement...

> 'It is necessary to choose one of the men who have been with us the whole time the Lord Jesus went in and out among us, beginning from John's baptism to the time when Jesus was taken up from us. For one of these must become a witness with us of his resurrection.' (Acts 1:21-22)

The man was to be an ear-witness to Jesus' teaching, from the beginning of His ministry at His baptism to the very end at His ascension; and he was to be an eye-witness to the risen Lord Jesus – someone who had actually seen Him in the flesh after the resurrection. Some of the women who had been with Jesus throughout would, probably, have fulfilled these criteria, but a man, Matthias, was chosen instead.

It's not that the apostles didn't appreciate the ministry of women; they just knew that they did not have the same function in the body as men. Paul, in particular, is often criticised for being very dismissive of women but, in fact, he endorsed and commended the ministry of women when it was exercised appropriately...

> I commend to you our sister Phoebe, a servant of the church in Cenchreae. I ask you to receive her in the Lord in a way worthy of the saints and to give her any help she may need from you, for she has been a great help to many people, including me. (Rom. 16:1-2)

> I plead with Euodia and I plead with Syntyche to agree with each other in the Lord. Yes, and I ask you, loyal yokefellow, help these women who have contended at my side in the cause of the gospel, along with Clement and the rest of my fellow workers, whose names are in the book of life. (Phil. 4:2-3)

> I have been reminded of your sincere faith, which first lived in your grandmother Lois and in your mother Eunice and, I am persuaded, now lives in you also. (2 Tim. 1:5)

But when it comes to determining what roles are appropriate for men and women in the life of the church, there are a number of passages that need to be considered.

1 Timothy 2:8-15

We should note the context of this passage. Paul is writing to Timothy, who has been left in charge of the church at Ephesus. He is particularly concerned about the reputation of the church and wants Christians to live consistently so the influence of the gospel spreads...

> I want men everywhere to lift up holy hands in prayer, without anger or disputing.
>
> I also want women to dress modestly, with decency and propriety, not with braided hair or gold or pearls or expensive clothes, but with good deeds, appropriate for women who profess to worship God. (1 Tim. 2:8-10)

Men are to pray and not quarrel. Prayer demonstrates their dependence on the Lord, but quarrelling destroys their unity with one another and leads to division. The church and the gospel lose credibility if Christians are always fighting one another. Women are to dress modestly and clothe themselves with good deeds appropriate for women who profess to know God. Where modesty and good deeds are absent, there are all kinds of unhelpful consequences, and the church's credibility is again affected.

Paul is also concerned that women understand that they do not have the same role as men within the church...

> A woman should learn in quietness and full submission. I do not permit a woman to teach or to have authority over a man; she must be silent. For Adam was formed first, then Eve. And Adam was not the one deceived; it was the woman who was deceived and became a sinner. But women will be saved through childbearing – if they continue in faith, love and holiness with propriety. (1 Tim. 2:11-15)

For a woman to be taught alongside a man was hugely significant, given the Jewish culture that tended to separate them. We have already seen how Jesus commended Mary for sitting at His feet and listening to Him. Here, Paul also anticipates that women will be taught alongside men, but he urges women to learn in quietness and submission, understanding that they do not have the same teaching role as men do. They are not forbidden to speak, as we shall see from 1 Corinthians, but a restless and aggressive attitude (the opposite of a quiet and submissive one) will, in the end, dishonour Christ and divide the church.

Paul then makes it clear that there are some contexts in which a woman should remain quiet. It is not appropriate for her to teach a man or have authority over him. In this context she must be silent, recognising that it is not an appropriate role for her as a woman. This cannot mean that women should never say anything to men in case they inadvertently teach them something! We have already seen that men and women can teach each other in more informal settings.[3] But Paul does say that it is inappropriate for a woman to teach a man in such a way that she exercises authority over him. That is not her role. This means that the teaching of the whole church, where men and women are gathered together to hear God's Word, is a role that is limited to men alone – and not even to all men. The criteria for appointing the male elders who have this task are pretty stringent.[4]

We should note that Paul does not argue this from the contemporary culture. It wasn't a ruling for the early church that is now obsolete for supposedly more enlightened generations. Nor does he argue it from

---

3   See, Ephesians 5:19-20 and Colossians 3:16.

4   See, for example, 1 Timothy 3:1-7 and Titus 1:5-9.

the Law of Moses, which because of Jesus' fulfilment of the Law didn't apply in quite the same way in the New Testament era. Paul doesn't argue his case in either of these ways. He argues it from creation. Men are to exercise authority in the church because God created them first! The created order needs to be upheld in the life of the local church. God wants the diversity of role within the body of Christ to be demonstrated alongside our unity in Him – as they are within the Godhead itself.

Verse 14 provides us with another reason. Whenever the created order is reversed, there is confusion, deception and chaos. When Eve rebelled against the created order, she was deceived by the serpent into thinking that eating the forbidden fruit was actually a good thing to do.[5] Adam also rebelled against the created order and ate the forbidden fruit, but he was not deceived – the implication being that he sinned openly, knowing that it was wrong.

I doubt this means that women are more gullible than men and therefore more likely to lead the church into error, although some people take that view. If that were really the case, then I can't see why other passages in Scripture would encourage women to teach women and children.[6] And why do Paul and the other apostles warn the early church so much about the false teachers, who were likely to lead them astray and who were, normally, men?[7] Eve's deception in the Garden certainly doesn't mean that men never get their doctrine wrong; they are just as likely to lead the church astray as women.

---

5   See Genesis 3:6.

6   See, for example, Proverbs 1:8, Proverbs 31:26, Acts 18:26, Titus 2:3-5, 2 Timothy 1:5.

7   See, for example, Acts 20:29-31, 2 Corinthians 11:1-7, Galatians 1:6-9, Colossians 2:8, 2:16-19, 1 Timothy 1:3-4, 1:18-20, 2 Timothy 2:16-18, 3:1-9, 4:3-4, 4:14-15, Titus 1:10-16, 2 Peter 2:1-12, 1 John 4:1-6, Jude 3-4.

Nevertheless, Eve's downfall does serve as an example that women should learn from – that when they reject the created order and take on roles that are not appropriate for them, they are vulnerable to Satan's deception. In exercising authority over men, they forfeit both the leadership and protection of men, and lay themselves open to all kinds of problems. They not only take on roles that are inappropriate but, by doing so, effectively prevent men from exercising their God-given role. In other words, sin has consequences, and when God's designated ordering of creation is ignored, there is chaos and all manner of other repercussions.

Verse 15 is complicated, but when we come across a verse that is hard to understand, it's good to eliminate what it *doesn't* mean in order to narrow down the options and discover what it *does* mean. It cannot mean that women are literally saved, in a redemptive sense, by having children. Women are saved through faith and by grace alone, just as men are.[8] Nor can it mean that godly women will be kept safe through labour. There are various examples in Scripture and throughout history of godly women who died in childbirth.[9] This is not a promise that Christian women are somehow immune from the tragic consequences of living in a broken world.

There are two more plausible explanations. One is that Paul is making reference to the birth of *the* child who brings salvation, that is, Jesus! He was born of a woman and fulfilled the promise that one of Eve's offspring would one day crush Satan's head, bringing salvation to all. Many people take this view, although it's hard to see why women are being singled out for salvation through this child, when men are also sinners and need to be saved by Christ.

---

8   See Ephesians 2:8-9.

9   For example, Rachel died giving birth to Benjamin (see Genesis 35:16-18).

So what does this verse mean? I think the most obvious explanation is that women restore the created order and are kept safe from Satan's deception if they embrace the unique role God has given them as child-bearers and do not take on inappropriate roles that He has reserved for men alone. But we need to be careful here: Paul is not saying that *all* women will be mothers, any more than he is saying that *all* men will be church elders – but they are both *unique* roles, the former given to some women and the latter to some men. In other words, both men and women need to understand that God has different roles for them to fulfil within the body of Christ and whenever these roles are blurred or ignored, the whole body suffers the consequences.

Objections

But, some will say, 'Hang on a minute. Is that really true? Surely, there are lots of churches in the UK and indeed across the world that are led by women with very obvious teaching gifts. There doesn't appear to be much confusion or disorder in them. And what about all the missionary women who took the gospel to India, Asia, and Africa? Surely, God did amazing things through them?' And, of course, the answer is, 'Yes, God did do amazing things through these women and continues to use women in the church today.' The issue is not one of gifting. No one would deny that women have considerable gifts, even teaching gifts. The issue is whether exercising them like this is God's preferred and revealed way of building up His church. It's hard to say this but, maybe, as a woman I am someone who can. We need to take a step back and see what impact women in positions of church leadership have had or are continuing to have on the church's ministry to men.

Most churches throughout the world are dominated by women. Most of them struggle to reach out to men. Why is that? It's my observation that where women are in the ascendancy, men take a step back. It's happened in Western society. It's happening in our churches. Whenever women are in positions of overall leadership in the church, the number of men in the congregation decreases over time. Men are driven out of the church if women are too prominent within it and won't be drawn into it if men are too scarce. The feminisation of the church has had a devastating impact on men, who often don't know what their role is anymore. This emasculation affects the way they lead (or fail to lead) their families, so their children grow up having no idea that the Lord wants them to embrace different gender roles within the family and the church.

Norman Rockwell, the American artist, encapsulates the problem well in this painting, which he calls 'Easter Morning'.[10]

---

10   Norman Rockwell, *Easter Morning* (May, 1959), www.globalgallery.com

There's little doubt in the artist's mind that church is really just for women and children, although the young boy at the back is clearly beginning to wonder why he has to go to church if Dad doesn't. It surely won't be long before he too will be planning his escape – a situation all too common in many households up and down the country each Sunday morning.

If the church is going to be at all credible for men in the twenty-first century, it needs to have more men at the heart of its leadership – men who value the unique role of women, and encourage it, while at the same time recognising their own unique role as men. The effectiveness of the church's ministry, both to men and to women, is at stake. While 1 Timothy 2 is clear that it is not appropriate for women to teach or have authority over men, this does not mean that they are to play no part in the meetings when God's people are gathered together.

1 Corinthians 11:3-16

Again, we need to note the context of this passage. Paul writes to the Corinthian church that he had planted to correct a variety of problems that had arisen since he left. In this section, he is particularly concerned about the need for good order in their church meetings...

> Now I want you to realise that the head of every man is Christ, and the head of the woman is man, and the head of Christ is God. Every man who prays or prophesies with his head covered dishonours his head. And every woman who prays or prophesies with her head uncovered dishonours her head – it is just as though her head were shaved. If a woman does not cover her head, she should have her hair cut off; and if it is a disgrace for a woman to have her hair

cut or shaved off, she should cover her head. A man ought
not to cover his head, since he is the image and glory of
God; but the woman is the glory of man. For man did not
come from woman, but woman from man; neither was man
created for woman, but woman for man. For this reason,
and because of the angels, the woman ought to have a sign
of authority on her head.

In the Lord, however, woman is not independent of man,
nor is man independent of woman. For as woman came
from man, so also man is born of woman. But everything
comes from God. Judge for yourselves: Is it proper for
a woman to pray to God with her head uncovered? Does
not the very nature of things teach you that if a man has
long hair, it is a disgrace to him, but that if a woman has
long hair, it is her glory? For long hair is given to her as
a covering. If anyone wants to be contentious about this,
we have no other practice – nor do the churches of God.
(1 Cor. 11:3-16)

Once again, there is remarkable freedom for women
here, freedom that is often overlooked. For women to
be able to pray and prophesy in public and with men
present went against all the normal Jewish conventions
of the day. But in the Christian church, it is entirely
appropriate for women to do these things. They are
redeemed in the same way as men and equally marked
out by the Spirit. The New Testament era introduces
new privileges for both men and women, as the Day of
Pentecost and fulfilment of Joel 2 show.[11]
    What Paul is concerned about is that men and
women need to demonstrate the created order when
they pray and prophesy in public. In other words, the
way they exercise these roles needs to be in accordance

---

11 See Acts 2:16-18.

with their gender. A man will do this by leaving his head uncovered. A woman will do this by making sure her head is covered, either by the wearing of a head-covering or by using her long hair as a covering on top of her head. By doing this she demonstrates that, as a woman, she is acting under authority and not usurping a man's role inappropriately.

Now, before we consider some of the cultural issues that might come into play here, it's worth noting that Paul again argues for this distinction from the created order. A man is to leave his head uncovered when he prays and prophesies because at the very beginning Adam did not come from Eve. A woman is to cover her head because, originally, Eve did come from Adam. Similarly, a man should leave his head uncovered because Adam was not made for Eve; a woman is to cover her head because Eve was made for Adam. The order of their creation is significant and needs to be visibly demonstrated if there is to be good order in the Church.

But notice too that Paul draws a comparison between the created order and the order of relationships within the Godhead. So God the Father is the head of Christ, Christ is the head of every man (in a generic sense, meaning the whole of humanity), and the husband is the head of his wife. A man who covers his head dishonours Christ, who is his head. Similarly, a woman who fails to cover her head dishonours her husband if she is married, or indeed, Christ who is her head even if she is not married. In other words, men show they are under the authority of Christ by leaving their heads uncovered, while women show they are under the authority of Christ (and their husbands if they are married) by covering their heads. They are both under the authority of Christ, but they are to demonstrate an understanding of their different gender roles in a visible way.

Culturally, the wearing of a head-covering may not have the same significance today. Certainly we know that in Ephesus women asserted themselves and worshipped the goddess Diana by keeping their hair down. Rebellious women and effeminate men, who worked as prostitutes in the temple of Diana, often had long, loose hair to advertise their trade. Given this background, we can see why Paul was so concerned that Christian men and women should not give off confusing signals about their gender either in their attitudes, their speech, or their actions.

But what does this all mean for us today? Of course, some denominations hold that women should wear head-coverings today. My problem with this is two-fold. First of all, the lack of a head-covering does not have the same connotation today as it did in the first century and secondly, churches who adopt this position often limit women to the extent that even with their heads covered they are not allowed to pray or prophesy. Jesus had some very harsh words for those who sought to uphold one area of the Law by conveniently negating another.[12]

But there are some denominations who ignore these instructions altogether, and that can't be right either. John Stott's distinction between the timeless principle and the cultural application of that principle is very helpful here.[13] On this basis, the timeless principle in this passage is the need for some

---

12   For example, the Corban rule attracted fierce criticism from Jesus (Mark 7:1-13).

13   See his essay on cultural transposition in *The Contemporary Christian* (John Stott, IVP, 1992).

gender distinction (based on the created order) and the cultural application of that timeless principle is the wearing/not wearing of head-coverings (which is culturally transitional). Western culture in the twenty-first century tends not to see head-coverings in the same way and short hair on a woman is not generally seen to be a sign of gender confusion, although long hair on a man can still be a little misleading. The wearing of an engagement ring and a wife taking her husband's surname are culturally accepted practices that perhaps provide some distinction between the sexes. Certainly, where a wife doesn't take her husband's surname, it can sometimes communicate a lack of submission to his authority and leadership in the marriage.

In any event, what is clear is that women were free to pray and prophesy in the gathered assembly (albeit in a way that didn't usurp men or communicate any lack of submission to their authority). Which then begs the question, what exactly is prophecy? Is it the same as preaching? Is it ever legitimate for a woman to preach, if it is clearly recognised that she does so under the authority of her husband and the male teaching elders? Some churches would certainly operate with this policy, and I know of several people who have been greatly encouraged by women who have preached from time to time under the authority of the male vicar or team leader. But, once again, the issue is not one of ability but of appropriateness. It is my considered view that 1 Corinthians 11:5 needs to be interpreted alongside the prohibition of 1 Timothy 2:12, so that whatever the women were doing when they prophesied, they weren't teaching or exercising authority over men.

The closest we get to discovering what prophecy actually involved comes a few chapters later where we read that...

> Everyone who prophesies speaks to men for their strength-
> ening, encouragement and comfort. He who speaks in
> a tongue edifies himself, but he who prophesies edifies the
> church. (1 Cor. 14:3-4)

On this basis it could be argued that testimonies, missionary reports, interviews, book reviews, news of summer camps and house-parties would all come under the umbrella of prophecy. In fact, anything that strengthens, encourages and edifies the church but falls short of preaching the Word of God to the gathered people of God would constitute prophesying. Of course, not everyone will agree with this, and there will always be a spectrum of opinions on this issue. Bible-believing Christians who seek to interpret Scripture in light of Scripture won't always draw the line in exactly the same place on secondary issues – and we will need to live with that, providing we accept that there are other ways of interpreting these passages (some more valid than others) and are careful not to trample over the consciences of others in asserting the legitimacy of our own views.[14]

1 Corinthians 14:26-40

While some would argue that Paul's affirmation in 1 Corinthians 11 that women can pray and prophesy in public contradicts or at least overrides his prohibition of women teaching men in 1 Timothy 2, it appears that Paul then contradicts himself again in 1 Corinthians 14!

---

14 As I write, the Church of England is in danger of making this a primary order issue in refusing to make any provision for those who cannot in good conscience accept the legislation allowing for the consecration of women bishops. I fear that this will mean that, in the years to come, agreeing to women bishops will become a test of orthodoxy for the progressive Church of England, while global Anglicanism will continue to see it as a second-order issue.

It seems as though he is now saying that women should remain silent in the churches and are not allowed to speak...

> What then shall we say, brothers? When you come together, everyone has a hymn, or a word of instruction, a revelation, a tongue or an interpretation. All of these must be done for the strengthening of the church. If anyone speaks in a tongue, two – or at the most three – should speak, one at a time, and someone must interpret. If there is no interpreter, the speaker should keep quiet in the church and speak to himself and God.
>
> Two or three prophets should speak, and the others should weigh carefully what is said. And if a revelation comes to someone who is sitting down, the first speaker should stop. For you can all prophesy in turn so that everyone may be instructed and encouraged. The spirits of prophets are subject to the control of prophets. For God is not a God of disorder but of peace.
>
> As in all the congregations of the saints, women should remain silent in the churches. They are not allowed to speak, but must be in submission, as the Law says. If they want to inquire about something, they should ask their own husbands at home; for it is disgraceful for a woman to speak in the church.
>
> Did the word of God originate with you? Or are you the only people it has reached? If anybody thinks he is a prophet or spiritually gifted, let him acknowledge that what I am writing to you is the Lord's command. If he ignores this, he himself will be ignored.
>
> Therefore, my brothers, be eager to prophesy, and do not forbid speaking in tongues. But everything should be done in a fitting and orderly way. (1 Cor. 14:26-40)

As with all passages of Scripture, we need to take note of the context. Paul is concerned about good order in the church because 'God is not a God of disorder but of peace' and 'Everything should be done in a fitting and orderly way.' Tongues, interpretation of tongues, a word of instruction or revelation must all be done in a way that promotes good order. Similarly, when people prophesy, they should do so in turn so that everyone can hear what is said. In this way, everyone will be instructed and encouraged.

So why are the women, who have been encouraged to pray and to prophesy a few chapters earlier, now told to remain silent? There are two possible explanations. One is that women are to remain silent during the weighing of prophecy. We know that prophecies were weighed by the elders of the church (who were all men), so that any heresy or wrong thinking could be filtered out. It could be that the women were to remain silent during this process – although presumably those men who were not elders would need to remain silent as well.

Perhaps a more probable explanation is in the limiting of interruptions during the meeting itself. Women are told to ask their husbands at home if there is something they don't understand – thereby affirming the husband's role as leader of the family but also ensuring that the public meetings didn't descend into chaos. Although the need for submission in this instance is argued from the law, Paul also appeals to the creation narratives to remind them that in the Garden of Eden the Word of God originally came to Adam (and not to Eve). Once again the created order must govern the church's practice and is, ultimately, a sign of submission to the Lord's will.

Over recent years, much of the debate concerning the role of women in the local church has focused on what they cannot do, and where these arguments are presented by overbearing men with little or no regard for the women in their congregations, it can lead to the women feeling they have no legitimate role to play – which then leads to either frustration or defeatism or both. But the truth is that women **are** needed because there is a role that only women can do. Men and women have different roles to play in the life of the local church, but both are needed if the people of God are to be discipled effectively.

Titus 2:1-10

Paul writes to Titus, who he has left on Crete, to appoint elders in the churches of every town. Having established the criteria that are to govern the appointment of these elders and reminded Titus of their role in guarding the truth and refuting error, Paul then urges him to teach the various groups within the church...

> You must teach what is in accord with sound doctrine. Teach the older men to be temperate, worthy of respect, self-controlled, and sound in faith, in love and in endurance.

> Likewise, teach the older women to be reverent in the way they live, not to be slanderers or addicted to much wine, but to teach what is good. Then they can train the younger women to love their husbands and children, to be self-controlled and pure, to be busy at home, to be kind, and to be subject to their husbands, so that no one will malign the word of God.

> Similarly, encourage the young men to be self-controlled. In everything set them an example by doing what is good. In your teaching show integrity, seriousness and soundness

of speech that cannot be condemned, so that those who oppose you may be ashamed because they have nothing bad to say about us.

Teach slaves to be subject to their masters in everything, to try to please them, not to talk back to them, and not to steal from them, but to show that they can be fully trusted, so that in every way they will make the teaching about God our Saviour attractive. (Titus 2:1-10)

What's interesting here is that, while Titus can teach the older men and older women, the younger men and the slaves, the specific teaching and training of younger women is left to the older women. That's not to say that men can't teach the whole Bible to women, far from it, but there is an important aspect of teaching, training and discipleship that only women can do. Titus can certainly teach women, but he cannot model what the Christian life looks like for a woman – he needs the older women to do it for him. Only they can model what it means to be a godly woman to other women.

Paul outlines three important areas of life that women need to have demonstrated to them by other women. First of all, in the area of their family lives, women need to be taught and trained to love their husbands and children, and to be subject to their husbands. Younger women need to learn from the examples of older godly women who can model this to them. It may seem strange to us that women need to be shown how to love their husbands and children – isn't it natural for women to demonstrate their nurturing instincts? Well, yes, to some extent – but also, no! Paul is no fool. He knows the default position of every heart is to look to our own interests, and women will not naturally love their husbands or their children in a totally selfless way. Nor will women naturally submit to their husband's authority – even if they know this is God's will for them. Many women can testify to the value of knowing, observing and learning from older women who demonstrate what it means to honour the Lord in the home.

Secondly, in the area of their moral lives, women need to be taught about purity and self-control, which, because they are women, will look slightly different to purity and self-control in men. It's no accident that where women are addressed directly in the New Testament, it is often in terms of what they wear and how they speak! That's because women often try to manipulate and gain power over men by either alluring them sexually or nagging them verbally. Modesty, purity and self-control are characteristics that don't come naturally to any woman, which is why it's so important for younger women to learn from the example of godly older women – who are reverent in the way they live and have learned to control their tongues!

And thirdly, in the area of their working lives, women need to be taught to be busy at home and kind. While our twenty-first century hackles may begin to rise at the thought of women being limited to working in the home (although the passage doesn't actually say that), Paul's emphasis here is far more likely to be on the need for them to be busy rather than specifically working at home. We are told in the previous chapter of Titus that Cretans are always liars, evil brutes and lazy gluttons,[15] so one way in which these women are to demonstrate the power of the gospel to change lives is in their productivity. No longer are they to lounge around the home indulging in gossip and gluttony! There is work to be done, and godly role models are needed to show how these young women are to engage in honest work. Nevertheless, we should not overlook the assumption that godly women will be home-focused in much of their work – and becoming a mother necessitates a change in priorities outside of the home.[16]

What's interesting about these instructions is the motivation that Paul gives for them. If women are not discipled in this way, then the Word of God is maligned. This shows that women have a vital role to play in the life of the local church, and where it is absent, the credibility of God's Word is at stake. He explains why in the next section of the letter...

> For the grace of God that brings salvation has appeared to all men. It teaches us to say 'No' to ungodliness and worldly passions, and to live self-controlled, upright and godly lives in this present age, while we wait for the blessed hope – the glorious appearing of our great God and Saviour, Jesus Christ, who gave himself for us to redeem us from all wickedness and to purify for himself a people that are his very own, eager to do what is good. (Titus 2:11-14)

It is the grace of God that saves us, but it is the grace of God that also transforms us. It teaches us

---

15   See Titus 1:12.

16   See 1 Timothy 5:11-14 for more on this.

to say 'no' to ungodly and worldly passions so the transforming power of the gospel can be seen in our lives. Men and women who have been redeemed by the Lord and are being purified by Him, will show this by the way they live, the way they conduct their relationships both at work and at home. What this means for men and women will be slightly different, which is why godly men and women are needed to teach and model it to them. Where this is done well, the gospel is seen to be very attractive and brings honour to the Lord.

These then are the passages that need to be considered when thinking about what roles are appropriate for men and women in the life of the local church. What's common to all of them is the need for good order, which demonstrates the unity and equality, but also the unparalleled diversity of the body of Christ – which itself reflects the relationships within the Godhead.

Egalitarian versus Complementarian patterns of leadership

How these passages are understood and interpreted in light of each other is hugely significant. What this means in practice varies enormously according to a whole spectrum of views. Most evangelical Christians would position themselves somewhere between the egalitarian left and the domineering right. And the different positions they hold are determined to some extent by the degree of emphasis they place on one New Testament passage over and against the others, as the following table attempts to show…

The Egalitarian Left	The Complementarian Middle			The Domineering Right
Men and women homogenised Differences masked	Men and women are equal in status, dignity and humanity but different roles in the church			Men more prominent Equality masked
Galatians 3:28 In Christ there is no male or female	1 Corinthians 11:3-16 Women can pray and prophesy under authority	Titus 2:3-5 Older women teach and train younger women	1 Timothy 2:11-15 Women should not teach or have authority over men	1 Corinthians 14:34-40 Women should remain silent in church & have no public role
Male and female presbyters (bishops, archbishops etc.)	Women can preach in certain contexts	Women are needed to disciple women	Women cannot preach to mixed groups	Women often frustrated and under-used in church

But someone might ask, 'Does it really matter if we hold an egalitarian or a complementarian position on the role of men and women in the church?' Well, yes, I think it does. Western society is becoming more and more egalitarian – not in the sense of seeing everyone as equal (which surely, we would agree with) but rather in the sense of seeing everyone as exactly the same (which I think we would dispute). But as this happens, there is also an unhealthy homogenisation that not only masks the God-given differences between men and women, but even tries to eradicate them.

So why is complementarianism so crucial for Christian discipleship? Because spiritual maturity in a woman looks slightly different than spiritual maturity in a man. As one writer puts it...

God has created men and women equal in status, dignity and humanity but He has also given them different roles in respect to one another. This balance between equality and difference means that some aspects of discipleship will be unisex while other aspects will be gender-specific.

It's easy to err in one direction or the other, – either by homogenising our conceptions of discipleship or by over-emphasising the differences. To be faithful to Genesis 1 and 2, as well as to all the relevant passages in the New Testament, a right perspective of Christian maturity is needed that will encourage models of male and female maturity that are both the same and different.

So every Christian, whether male or female, needs to live a life of repentance and faith. Every Christian needs to grow in the knowledge of God and conformity to Jesus Christ. Every Christian needs to be united to the fellowship of believers. But if that's all a church Sunday school, youth group, small group Bible study and weekly sermons teach about Christian discipleship, then they will have implicitly smothered the God-intended differences between men and women, and thus misrepresented 'maturity.'[17]

If complementary patterns of leadership, in the family or in the church, are ignored, then one of two things will happen. Either men will so dominate and frustrate women that the women become doormats, or women will usurp men and take on inappropriate roles that make the men wimp out and sit back. This then results in churches full of aggressive men and passive women on the one hand or masculine women and effeminate men on the other – and neither are attractive to outsiders or honouring to the Lord Jesus. What's more, the transforming power of the gospel is masked as

---

17   Jonathan Leeman, 'Why complementarianism is crucial to disciple-ship' (9 Marks eJournal, July/Aug 2010, Volume 7, Issue 3).

Christian men and women appear to be little different from their unbelieving peers.

My advice to Emily, as she struggled to withstand the pressure to take on roles that are inappropriate for her as a woman, was simple. She needs to delight in the wonderful diversity of the body of Christ. The Lord has graciously gifted her with Bible teaching skills, but He wants her to use them in a way that adorns His gospel and makes it attractive to others. What He needs her to do is to teach, train and model the Christian life, as a woman, to other women – and to stop worrying if she doesn't have the same work capacity as her male colleagues. Understanding who she is in Christ and what role she has in the body of Christ does not limit her effectiveness in ministry but rather liberates her to be the woman God wants her to be and to do the work He's given her to do.

But what about the role of women in society? Does God's design for men and women mean that there are some roles outside the family and the church that are off-limits for women? To what extent should we apply the created order to the workplace in general? These and other related questions are the subject of the next chapter.

DISCUSSION QUESTIONS FOR GROUPS/INDIVIDUALS

1. How does the New Testament affirm the equality of men and women?

2. How does the created order define the types of roles men and women are to have in the local church?

3. What roles are unique to men and what roles are unique to women? How are they related?

4. How do complementarian patterns of leadership counteract the tendencies towards either over-assertive men and passive women or masculine women and effeminate men leading our churches?

5. How can we better encourage the ministry of older women to teach, train and model the Christian life to younger women?

9

The Implications
of God's design for the workplace

Wei Ling is 38 and works as a doctor in General Practice. When I first met her, nearly fifteen years ago, she was a medical student at university who had high hopes of becoming a hospital consultant. Her grades were very good and she had the necessary drive and ambition to put in the long hours to achieve her goal. Her particular field of interest was paediatrics and, for a while, everything seemed to be going very well. After university, she moved to London to start her clinical training and stayed on at one of the London hospitals to complete her house jobs. She then took some time out to do a PhD, and after three years got a job as a paediatric registrar in north London. But it was during the next couple of years that things started to go seriously wrong. This is how she describes what happened...

> I was working in a very male dominated department and
> had to work twice as hard as everyone else or no-one would

take me seriously. The hours were long and I was working for a consultant who had a very aggressive style of management and treated everyone around him with contempt. What made things worse was the realisation that he seemed to favour those who treated others just as badly. The junior doctors thought he was wonderful and enjoyed joining him in the heavy drinking sessions that went on after work.

It was a pretty negative working environment all round but the last straw came when I completely lost it with one of the team and bawled them out for forgetting to run some tests on a patient. The consultant praised me for asserting myself and taking control, something he had previously thought I would never be able to do. It was then that I realised I was becoming the battleaxe I'd always feared I'd become. That wasn't what I'd gone into medicine for but it seemed I couldn't advance in that team without taking on the some of the more unattractive male characteristics of its leader.

I wasn't prepared to do that and, in the absence of any other paediatric registrar posts, decided to re-train as a GP instead. The hours are better and the working environment more congenial. I take my hat off to the women who have made it to consultant because I think the medical profession really needs them, but I fear the physical and emotional demands of getting there were just too high for me.[1]

Whatever you think of Wei Ling's reasons for leaving hospital medicine, her experience does raise questions about the different ways in which men and women go about their work, and whether there are some jobs that are just more suited for men.[2] One would hope that

---

1   From a letter I received from Wei Ling in October 2008.

2   There are more male consultants than female consultants, more male judges than female judges, more female GPs than male GPs and more female teachers than male teachers.

the consultant she worked for was not typical in the way he managed his team, although incidents like this are, sadly, not that unusual. Nevertheless, there will be others who provide a much more positive working environment for their colleagues, but where women have taken on these roles it is also true that, in many cases, they have had to adopt a more 'male' style of leadership in order to get there.

Of course, not all men are aggressive in the way that they lead their teams, and we should be careful not to resort to unhelpful stereotypes. But then, women are often considered not to have the necessary qualities to lead a team precisely because they are too nice, or too passive, or too gentle, and therefore lack the decisive cutting-edge mentality that is needed for making tough decisions and not worrying about the effect it may have on rest of the team. This leads one writer to observe that...

> We must reckon with the possibility that in the various spheres of life it is possible that role relationships emerge for men and women that so deeply compromise what a man or woman senses is appropriate for their masculine or feminine personhood that they have to seek a different position.[3]

So, some would argue that men are more suited to these kinds of leadership roles just by virtue of the fact that they are men, and, by implication, that women are less suited to these roles just because they are women. As another writer puts it...

---

3   Wayne Grudem, 'A Vision of Biblical Complementarity' in *Recovering Biblical Manhood and Womanhood* edited by John Piper and Wayne Grudem (Crossway, 1991).

> While I am not keen on hierarchy and patriarchy as terms describing the man-woman relationship in Scripture, passages like Genesis 2:18-25 and Ephesians 5:21-33 continue to convince me that the man-woman relationship is intrinsically non-reversible. By this I mean that, other things being equal, a situation in which a female boss has a male secretary, or a marriage in which the woman (as we say) wears the trousers, will put more strain on the humanity of both parties than if it were the other way round. This is part of the reality of the creation, a given fact that nothing will change.[4]

But not everyone is convinced by this. For example, the passages cited in this quote are both referring to marriage, where there are clearly defined roles for husbands and wives. But to extend these parameters into other contexts is, surely, to go beyond what the Bible is actually saying. It also seems strange to me that while, on the one hand, some people say that women should submit to all men just by virtue of the fact that they are women and have a subordinate role, they are never heard to say, on the other hand, that men should sacrificially love all women just by virtue of the fact that they are women and need protecting! We should be careful not to read into Scripture things that are simply not there. A wife is to submit to her husband and not to every man she knows. A husband is to sacrificially love his wife and not every woman he knows. To do otherwise belittles the privileges and responsibilities of marriage, let alone the intimacy and exclusivity of their relationship.[5]

---

4   J. I. Packer, 'Understanding the differences,' in *Women, Authority and the Bible,* edited by Alvera Mickelsen (Downers Grove: IVP, 1986).

5   My thanks to Vicky Hordern for her helpful comments and observations on this.

We have already seen that the created order is significant in determining what roles are suitable for men and women within the nuclear family and within the church family – but to what extent should God's design for men and women impact the roles they take outside of these familial contexts? Does the created order have anything to say on how we should structure society? Is it possible for women to take on positions of responsibility over men without becoming pseudo-men in the process? While none of these issues are addressed specifically in the Bible (indicating, perhaps, a degree of freedom in this area), there are nevertheless a number of passages that should be taken into account...

GENESIS 1:26-28 – THE CREATION MANDATE

Then God said, 'Let us make man in our image, in our likeness, and let them rule over the fish of the sea and the birds of the air, over the livestock, over all the earth, and over all the creatures that move along the ground.'

So God created man in his own image,
  in the image of God he created him;
  male and female he created them.

God blessed them and said to them, 'Be fruitful and increase in number; fill the earth and subdue it. Rule over the fish of the sea and the birds of the air and over every living creature that moves on the ground.'

The creation mandate to fill the earth and subdue it is dependent on both men and women playing their part. Both are made in the image of God and as such are His chosen representatives to rule over the rest of creation. There is no suggestion here that it is only

Adam who is to rule over the creation or the men who follow him. The mandate is given to both Adam and Eve ('let them rule') and to the men and women who come after them. This means that there is no intrinsic reason why women shouldn't be farmers, botanists, zoologists, medics, lawyers, teachers and councillors – and so take part in the subduing of creation that is both their privilege and, indeed, their responsibility.

It is true that women are not as strong as men physically,[6] and becoming a mother will necessitate a change in a woman's priorities, but to exclude her from certain roles in the secular workplace just because she is a woman seems unreasonable and is surely a denial of her humanity and contravenes the creation mandate. When men and women enter into a covenant relationship either when they marry or join the community of believers, there are certain parameters in place that will enable them to model the glorious diversity of role within those contexts – and become a visual aid either of the relationship Christ has with the church in the first instance, or the unity and diversity of the Godhead in the second. But where these covenant (or familial) relationships are absent, there is freedom.

Judges 4:4-10 – Deborah

> Deborah, a prophetess, the wife of Lappidoth, was leading
> Israel at that time. She held court under the Palm of Deborah
> between Ramah and Bethel in the hill country of Ephraim,
> and the Israelites came to her to have their disputes decided.
> She sent for Barak son of Abinoam from Kedesh in Naphtali
> and said to him, 'The Lord, the God of Israel, commands

---

6   See, for example, 1 Peter 3:7.

you: "Go, take with you ten thousand men of Naphtali and Zebulun and lead the way to Mount Tabor. I will lure Sisera, the commander of Jabin's army, with his chariots and his troops to the Kishon River and give him into your hands."'

Barak said to her, 'If you go with me, I will go; but if you don't go with me, I won't go.'

'Very well,' Deborah said, 'I will go with you. But because of the way you are going about this, the honour will not be yours, for the Lord will hand Sisera over to a woman.' So Deborah went with Barak to Kedesh, where he summoned Zebulun and Naphtali. Ten thousand men followed him, and Deborah also went with him.

Deborah is often championed by evangelical feminists as a prime example of a woman whose leadership role in Israel was endorsed and blessed by God. On this basis they argue that it is entirely appropriate for women to exercise authority over men in the church – sidelining Paul's prohibition in 1 Timothy 2 as either cultural (appealing to a specific situation in Ephesus at the time) or uncanonical (thereby undermining the authority of Scripture and their claim to be evangelically orthodox).

While it is hard to draw clear principles from narrative (on that basis we could argue for the legitimacy of polygamy, the setting up of pagan shrines, and the use of prostitutes), a closer inspection of the text reveals that Deborah actually affirms male leadership over God's people rather than her own! We're told in this passage that she was a prophetess and a judge, but the way she exercised these roles was decidedly different to the way men exercised them. So, while Jeremiah, Isaiah and all the other prophets in Israel exercised a public ministry when they proclaimed the word of the Lord, Deborah did not prophesy in public. Instead, her prophetic role seems to be limited to private and individual instruction.

Similarly, the judging role she had seems to have been conducted in private, and she did not lead the people of Israel into battle as the other judges did. In fact, she refused to lead the people militarily and insisted that it was Barak's role rather than hers. When he refused unless she went with him, she rebuked him for his cowardice and dishonourable conduct – indicating that he should have acted like a man and led the people into battle on his own. So, rather than asserting leadership and authority for herself, Deborah actually affirms the rightness of male leadership.

But that's not all. The passage seems also to affirm that the settling of disputes through arbitration and judicial decisions was an entirely appropriate role for a woman provided that the way she went about it didn't compromise or usurp the leadership of men. Perhaps on this basis Deborah can be seen as a positive role model for any female lawyers, teachers and councillors who go about their work with wisdom and competence while also recognising that, in the home and in the church, they do not have the same authority as their husbands or their church leaders.

PROVERBS 31:10-31 – THE NOBLE WIFE

If ever we need to see what a wise and godly woman looks like in practice, we need look no further than the noble wife of Proverbs 31. Here we have a supreme example of a satisfied and contented wife and mother who rejoices in the Lord's goodness and organises her time with selfless efficiency. While she has clearly made the home a priority, it would appear that her children are now grown up or, at least, are less dependent than they were. She therefore finds herself at the stage of life where work outside the home can take more prominence. The variety of different roles described here is simply breath-taking…

> A wife of noble character who can find?
>> She is worth far more than rubies.
>
> Her husband has full confidence in her
>> and lacks nothing of value.
>
> She brings him good, not harm,
>> all the days of her life.
>
> She selects wool and flax
>> and works with eager hands.
>
> She is like the merchant ships,
>> bringing her food from afar.
>
> She gets up while it is still dark;
>> she provides food for her family
>> and portions for her servant girls.
>
> She considers a field and buys it;
>> out of her earnings she plants a vineyard.
>
> She sets about her work vigorously;
>> her arms are strong for her tasks.
>
> She sees that her trading is profitable,
>> and her lamp does not go out at night.
>
> In her hand she holds the distaff
>> and grasps the spindle with her fingers.
>
> She opens her arms to the poor
>> and extends her hands to the needy.
>
> When it snows, she has no fear for her household;
>> for all of them are clothed in scarlet.
>
> She makes coverings for her bed;
>> she is clothed in fine linen and purple.
>
> Her husband is respected at the city gate,
>> where he takes his seat among the elders of the land.

She makes linen garments and sells them,
  and supplies the merchants with sashes.
She is clothed with strength and dignity;
  she can laugh at the days to come.
She speaks with wisdom,
  and faithful instruction is on her tongue.
She watches over the affairs of her household
  and does not eat the bread of idleness.
Her children arise and call her blessed;
  her husband also, and he praises her:
'Many women do noble things,
  but you surpass them all.'
Charm is deceptive, and beauty is fleeting;
  but a woman who fears the Lord is to be praised.
Give her the reward she has earned,
  and let her works bring her praise at the city gate.

The secret to this woman's contentment is a right fear of the Lord – fear in the sense of reverence and awe rather than alarm or trepidation. Throughout the wisdom literature the writers affirm that a fear of the Lord is the beginning of wisdom,[7] and here the noble wife is the epitome of a wise woman. So, the Lord is at the centre of everything she does and enables her to honour her husband, provide for her children, watch over her household, develop prudence and good stewardship, give to the poor, run her own business and prepare for the future. She is able to laugh at the days to come because she knows she is eternally secure. She has learned to trust the Lord in any and every circumstance, and her gentle and quiet spirit has earned her a good reputation with outsiders – even her

---

7   See, for example, Job 28:28, Psalm 111:10, Proverbs 1:7 and Ecclesiastes 12:13.

husband's colleagues marvel at her good works. She is quite a woman.

What makes her so attractive is her love for the Lord first and foremost, but also her desire to serve Him in whatever she does. She clearly relates very well with people both inside and outside of the home. There's no competitiveness, no malice, no aggression, no distress – but rather kindness, gentleness, thoughtfulness and poise. There's no gossip, no slander, no laziness, no bitterness but reverence, compassion, busyness and joy. A woman like this would be an asset to any team and a pleasure to work with.

The different roles she takes on outside of the home show there are any number of jobs a woman can have. Many of them would have involved working with men and in some instances having authority over them, but she doesn't squash them or manipulate them. Neither does she usurp or undermine her husband but understands that her role in the marriage is different to his. As an elder in the land he has responsibilities outside of the home that she cannot have, but she doesn't appear to be remotely worried about that but gives herself wholeheartedly to the work the Lord has given her to do. She doesn't appear to begrudge the time spent with the children and clearly has a wonderful relationship with them. Here is a woman who understands the different roles God has assigned to her and fulfils them with joy and contentment.

Acts 16:11-15 – Lydia

From Troas we put out to sea and sailed straight for Samothrace, and the next day on to Neapolis. From there we travelled to Philippi, a Roman colony and the leading city of that district of Macedonia. And we stayed there several days.

On the Sabbath we went outside the city gate to the river, where we expected to find a place of prayer. We sat down and began to speak to the women who had gathered there. One of those listening was a woman named Lydia, a dealer in purple cloth from the city of Thyatira, who was a worshipper of God. The Lord opened her heart to respond to Paul's message. When she and the members of her household were baptized, she invited us to her home. 'If you consider me a believer in the Lord,' she said, 'come and stay at my house.' And she persuaded us.

We don't know much about Lydia, and it is, once again, rather difficult to make hard and fast principles out of narrative, but what we do know is quite revealing. Whether she was a widow or had never married we don't know but she made her living from dealing in purple cloth. Originally from Thyatira (where one of the letters to the seven churches was sent in Revelation), she had settled in Philippi, one of the busiest trade centres in ancient Greece. Undoubtedly, her work would have involved working with men and as a dealer of purple cloth, not just a weaver or seller, she evidently ran quite a large business. She was a devout worshipper of God and as such would have met to pray with other Jews outside the city gate, which was the usual practice in towns and cities where there were no synagogues.

It was at this place of prayer that she first met the Apostle Paul and heard the gospel of grace. The Lord opened her heart to believe the message and she was baptised, together with her whole household. And to show the depth of her commitment to the Lord she persuaded Paul and the rest of his team to stay with her. She was a woman of influence, who had her own business, her own property and ran a large household – which presumably meant she was also quite wealthy. But there's no suggestion from the text that the way she lived or worked was at all inappropriate for her as a woman. Critics may say that it's hard to argue this point when the text doesn't either confirm or deny any approval, but it seems that Paul had no problem with it and graciously accepted her offer of hospitality.

ROMANS 16:1-2 – PHOEBE

We looked briefly at Paul's commendation of Phoebe in chapter eight but it is worthy of closer scrutiny here. Paul is often maligned for his negative attitude towards women, but he was not a misogynist and greatly valued the work they did...

> I commend to you our sister Phoebe, a servant of the church in Cenchreae. I ask you to receive her in the Lord in a way worthy of the saints and to give her any help she may need from you, for she has been a great help to many people, including me.

Phoebe is called both a sister and a servant, indicating that she was not just a member of the church in Cenchreae (to the southeast of Corinth), but an active participant in it. Put simply, she loved the Lord and so served His church, which is one of the authenticating signs of deep and sincere conversion.[8] The word for servant is *diakonos* or 'deacon,' but commentators argue as to whether or not this was a formally recognised position of leadership in the church. Was Phoebe the

---

8   See, for example, John 13:35, 1 John 2:9-11 and 1 John 3:16-20.

first woman deacon of the early church? I'm not sure it really matters. The point is that she *belonged* to the household of faith and *served* the people of God. She was a true servant – what she believed was borne out by how she behaved.

Paul commends her because she has been a great help to many people, including him. The extent of her help is mentioned as well as the degree. She was helpful in extent, in that she helped many people, and helpful in degree, in that she was a great help to all of them. It's interesting that Paul uses the word 'help' here. Phoebe was a helper, not a leader, implying perhaps that she understood the distinctive role she had as a woman in the life of the local church. She doesn't appear to have been a threat to Paul in any way but was greatly valued by him and the church where she served. She had proven herself again and again – both in her reliability and her consistency. Indeed, Paul includes himself in the number of people who she has helped and now, as she carries this letter to Rome, she is being a great help to him again.

Note, too, how the Christians were to receive Phoebe when she arrived in Rome – in a manner worthy of the saints. They were to treat her well and to honour her service of the Lord and of them. Receiving Phoebe in this way was tantamount to receiving Paul himself and the Lord Jesus, who had commissioned him.[9] She was a reliable servant but she was not aloof or self-sufficient. She needed them too and would have been dependent on them for food and shelter. She was keen to serve her brothers and sisters in Rome but she wasn't too proud to receive the help that they could give her too.

---

9   See, for example, Matthew 10:40-42.

My reason for including Phoebe here is that she is just one of many examples of women in the Bible who worked hard in their service of the Lord, in practical and not 'upfront' ways. Our Western culture tends to equate work with employment, but this is not the Bible's view. There is much work to be done in the service of the gospel by both men and women. Some will serve in more upfront ways but many will work quietly in the background. There is no end to the work that needs to be done and no suggestion here that Phoebe, as a woman, was ill-equipped for this important task. We don't know if she had business in Rome and often travelled there, but her willingness to take this letter, no doubt at some cost to herself, was a great service to the church – both to the church in Rome at the time and to every generation of believers since then.

IMPLICATIONS FOR US TODAY

These then are just some of the passages that need to be considered when determining whether God's design for men and women has any implications for the workplace. The creation mandate seems to open up a multitude of roles and responsibilities that men and woman can share as together they subdue the earth and rule over the rest of creation. Within the familial or covenant contexts of marriage and the church, there is a diversity of role that demonstrates the relationships within the covenant community of God Himself – but the parameters of that diversity are not binding where there are no covenant relationships in place.

Caroline Spencer, writing for the City Bible Forum in Sydney, makes this point very well when she says…

> The corporate world is not a familial relationship. Certainly
> God loves the world and there is a sense that mankind stands

in indirect relationship with Him in creation, but familial relationship requires redemption. Nor is the corporate workplace interested in teaching the things of God.

If in the Bible the link is between teaching and authority in familial relationships, then it is difficult to see how headship could be definitively applied in the corporate world. The authority or leadership that is exercised in the corporate workplace is of a different order to the headship that is part of the Bible's teaching on gender and roles.[10]

IN NON-FAMILIAL CONTEXTS, IT'S NOT WHAT YOU DO, IT'S HOW YOU DO IT

While Scripture doesn't specifically tackle the issue of what roles men and women can take outside the home (which leads many to assume that there is a degree of freedom in this area), what is addressed time and time again is how people should conduct themselves – even to the point of suffering for doing what is right in God's eyes…

Bless those who persecute you; bless and do not curse. Rejoice with those who rejoice; mourn with those who mourn. Live in harmony with one another. Do not be proud, but be willing to associate with people of low position. Do not be conceited. Do not repay anyone evil for evil. Be careful to do what is right in the eyes of everybody. If it is possible, as far as it depends on you, live at peace with everyone. (Rom. 12:14-18)

Do not let any unwholesome talk come out of your mouths, but only what is helpful for building others up according to their needs, that it may benefit those who listen. And do not grieve the Holy Spirit of God, with whom you were

10   Caroline Spencer, 'Christian women and corporate leadership' (City Bible Forum, April 2010).

sealed for the day of redemption. Get rid of all bitterness, rage and anger, brawling and slander, along with every form of malice. Be kind and compassionate to one another, forgiving each other, just as in Christ God forgave you. (Eph. 4:29-32)

Do nothing out of selfish ambition or vain conceit, but in humility consider others better than yourselves. Each of you should look not only to your own interests, but also to the interests of others. (Phil. 2:3-4)

Make it your ambition to lead a quiet life, to mind your own business and to work with your hands, just as we told you, so that your daily life may win the respect of outsiders and so that you will not be dependent on anybody. (1 Thess. 4:11-12)

Submit yourselves for the Lord's sake to every authority instituted among men: whether to the king, as the supreme authority, or to governors, who are sent by him to punish those who do wrong and to commend those who do right. For it is God's will that by doing good you should silence the ignorant talk of foolish men. Live as free men, but do not use your freedom as a cover-up for evil; live as servants of God. Show proper respect to everyone: Love the brotherhood of believers, fear God, honour the king. (1 Pet. 2:13-17)

Slaves, submit yourselves to your masters with all respect, not only to those who are good and considerate, but also to those who are harsh. For it is commendable if a man bears up under the pain of unjust suffering because he is conscious of God. But how is it to your credit if you receive a beating for doing wrong and endure it? But if you suffer for doing good and you endure it, this is commendable before God. (1 Pet. 2:18-20)

None of these passages are addressed to men alone. Women too have the responsibility of behaving well, even to the point of suffering for doing what is right in God's eyes. The creation mandate opens up a wide variety of roles for both men and women who are made in His image and have delegated rule in His world. But these passages indicate that the Lord is perhaps more concerned about how we do them than what we do, how we work rather than where we work, how we make progress in developing godly character rather than chalking up an impressive CV.

Women are free to exercise authority and rule over men in secular work contexts, providing the way they do so adorns the gospel and doesn't undermine or usurp the authoritative role those men may have in other contexts. In other words, the way men and women lead their teams needs to be in line with the godly character that is expected from all God's people and not by throwing their weight around or by satisfying their selfish ambitions. But women need to be mindful of the fact that the men on their teams may have positions of authority in other contexts, ones that they do not share, for example as husbands and fathers and in some cases as church elders, and should be careful not to undermine, demean or emasculate them. Male headship may not apply to the secular workplace but it should still be respected and upheld – because it does apply in other contexts.

We need to keep fighting sin and acknowledge that the workplace is often one of the fiercest battlegrounds. Whether it's sexual temptation or gossip or the need to prove ourselves or get even with more unscrupulous colleagues, the battle with sin is very real. But so is the battle of the sexes. Men will be tempted to abuse and dominate women harshly, women will be tempted to manipulate them and control them in more subtle ways – either by alluring them sexually or by manipulating them verbally.

Christian men in positions of leadership in the secular workplace and in familial relationships with men and women in other contexts may want to ask themselves the following questions...[11]

- In relating to Miss X on my team, am I feeding my desire to dominate and control her?

- Did the way I led that meeting encourage Mrs Y or squash and humiliate her?

- How can I help the women on my team to take the initiative without patronising them?

- What sort of model of leadership am I presenting to the men on my team?

- How can I encourage the men and women on my team to take their family responsibilities seriously?

- How is my leadership role impacting the way I relate to my wife at home?

- How is my leadership role impacting the way I relate to the elders in my church?

- How can I encourage the husbands in my homegroup to lead their wives?

Similarly, Christian women in positions of leadership in the secular workplace and in familial relationships with men and women in other contexts may want to ask themselves the following questions...

---

11   My thanks to Annie Sellheim for her helpful comments and suggestions in compiling these questions.

- In relating to Mr X on my team, am I feeding my desire to dominate and control him?

- Did the way I led that meeting encourage Mr Y or squash and humiliate him?

- How can I help the men on my team to take the initiative without competing with them?

- What sort of model of leadership am I presenting to the women on my team?

- How can I encourage the men and women on my team to take their family responsibilities seriously?

- How is my leadership role impacting the way I relate to my husband at home?

- How is my leadership role impacting the way I relate to the elders in my church?

- How can I encourage the wives in my homegroup to submit to their husbands?

The challenge for all God's people is to honour and serve the Lord in the workplace, whatever it may be, and to resist temptation, living lives that have been transformed by the power of the Spirit. Only then will our working relationships be as God intended. Only then will we…

> '…live such good lives among the pagans that though they accuse you of doing wrong, they may see your good deeds and glorify God on the day he visits us.' (1 Pet. 2:12)

We have seen how God's design for men and women has implications for marriage, and the church, and while not binding in the workplace still has an impact on the way we relate to men and women, who will have diverse roles in other contexts. But what about the

New Creation, where everything is perfected? To what extent does God's design for men and women still hold and what will it look like in practice? These are the questions we'll be considering in the next chapter.

DISCUSSION QUESTIONS FOR GROUPS/INDIVIDUALS

1. What typically characterizes a more negative model of leadership in the workplace? In what ways have we been encouraged to adopt these characteristics ourselves?

2. What does the creation mandate have to say about the different types of work that men and women can do outside the home and the church?

3. To what extent do the complementary roles of men and women in marriage and the church determine the roles they can take outside of those contexts?

4. To what extent do the complementary roles of men and women in marriage and the church impact the way we relate to and treat men and women in the workplace?

5. What attitudes and behaviour in the workplace do we need to change in light of this chapter?

10

The Perfection of God's design

In my study at home I have two photos of my godson, Phil. One is a school photo taken when he was seven. He'd recently lost two of his front teeth, so the toothless grin makes him look even more impish than normal. The other photo was taken five months ago on the day he left for the States to study for a year as part of his BA in American Studies. The impish grin is still there, but he now has a full set of teeth. While he's been away we've emailed and Skyped a few times and, although I'd love to fly over to California to visit him, it's unlikely that I'll see him until he returns to the UK in the summer.

While he's in the States, I could carry Phil's most recent photo around with me to remind me of what he looks like and use the Internet to communicate with him, but neither will be necessary when he's home and I can see him face to face. In fact, it would be really odd if, when he's back in the UK, I related only to the photo of Phil instead of to Phil himself, or tried to access him via the Internet when he's sitting on the other side of the kitchen table. The things that are helpful reminders and even pointers to Phil while he's absent will be completely redundant when he's present. Useful though the photo and the Internet are, they are no substitutes for the real Phil!

This begins to illustrate, at least to some extent, the difference between life in this present age and life in the age to come. It's not a perfect illustration but, in some respects, life in the present is like the period of time that I'm in now – where the photo of Phil and the Internet are really useful pointers to Phil, but life in the age to come will be more tangible and much more significant, like the time when he returns. C.S. Lewis famously described life in the here and now as the shadow-lands and life in the world to come as reality. While we are here in the shadow-lands, there are various pointers that can help us to understand a little of what life will be like in reality, but when that time comes these pointers will cease to be useful or indeed necessary.

One of the pointers to the age to come that will one day be redundant is marriage. Throughout the Bible, marriage is seen to be a precious gift from the Lord – in fact, marriage was His idea at the very beginning. Children also, are a wonderful blessing from Him. But, in the world to come, both marriage and family life as we know them will cease to be important or necessary because the realities to which they have been pointing are more tangible and much more significant. This means that despite what the popular culture thinks, husbands and wives are *not* re-united after their deaths, at least not as husband and wife. Christian husbands and wives will not be re-united as husband and wife in the age to come. Instead they will relate as brother and sister. Similarly, Christian parents and children in this life won't be re-united as parents and children in the next, as they too will relate as brothers and sisters. The pointers of marriage and family life in the shadow-lands give way and are superseded by the perfected reality of just one family – the family of God.

John Piper makes this point well in his excellent book *This Momentary Marriage…*

> There is no human marriage after death. The shadow of covenant-keeping between husband and wife gives way to the reality of covenant-keeping between Christ and His glorified Church. Nothing is lost. The music of every pleasure is transposed into an infinitely higher key.[1]

> My father had a thirty-six-year marriage with my mother and, after her death, a twenty-five-year marriage with my step-mother. But in the resurrection, the shadow gives way to the reality. My father will not be married in heaven, either to my mother or my step-mother. Marriage is a pointer toward the glory of Christ and the church. But in the resurrection the pointer vanishes into the perfection of that glory.[2]

This means that earthly marriage should never be viewed as an end in itself, because God always intended it to be a pointer to a far greater reality. Jesus taught that marriage was instituted by God and uniquely united a man and a woman for the duration of their earthly lives together, but He also made it clear that the union of marriage between a husband and a wife does not continue beyond death…

---

1   John Piper, *This Momentary Marriage* (IVP, 2009), p. 14.

2   Ibid., p. 52.

'At the beginning of creation God made them male and female. "For this reason a man will leave his father and mother and be united to his wife, and the two will become one flesh." So they are no longer two, but one. Therefore what God has joined together, let man not separate.' (Mark 10:6-9)

'At the resurrection, people will neither marry nor be given in marriage; they will be like the angels in heaven.' (Matt. 22:30)

The Apostle Paul taught that the only marriage in heaven is the marriage between Christ and His bride, the church. In fact, the whole of his ministry could be described as, first of all, inviting people to participate in the marriage between Christ and the church, and then preparing them for the heavenly wedding banquet. It's not that our union with Christ hasn't begun in the here and now, far from it, but the consummation of that union will not be realised in this life. Now we see Him only in part. Then we will see Him face to face...

I have been crucified with Christ and I no longer live, but Christ lives in me. The life I live in the body, I live by faith in the Son of God, who loved me and gave himself for me. (Gal. 2:20)

I am jealous for you with a godly jealousy. I promised you to one husband, to Christ, so that I might present you as a pure virgin to him. But I am afraid that just as Eve was deceived by the serpent's cunning, your minds may somehow be led astray from your sincere and pure devotion to Christ. (2 Cor. 11:2-3)

Husbands, love your wives, just as Christ loved the church and gave himself up for her to make her holy, cleansing her by the washing with water through the word, and to present

her to himself as a radiant church, without stain or wrinkle
or any other blemish, but holy and blameless. (Eph. 5:25-27)

When perfection comes, the imperfect disappears. When
I was a child, I talked like a child, I thought like a child,
I reasoned like a child. When I became a man, I put childish
ways behind me. Now we see but a poor reflection as in
a mirror; then we shall see face to face. Now I know in
part; then I shall know fully, even as I am fully known.
(1 Cor. 13:8-12)

But what will heaven be like? Given that we are
still bound by time and have only ever experienced
life in a fallen and broken world, where sin and its
consequences are all too evident, it can be hard for us
to understand what life will be like in the new creation.
Scripture uses a variety of metaphors to try and explain
it, but because these metaphors are trying to describe the
indescribable and help us imagine the unimaginable,
the picture they give us is always incomplete.

Broadly speaking, life in the new creation can be
described in two ways...

The renewal of all things

Everything will be made new. The heavens and the
earth, the created order, the animals, our bodies, our
relationships, our experience of life, of work, and of
God will all be made new. Everything will be perfect.
Life will be better than we could possibly imagine and
even better than it was before the Fall...

Behold, I will create
   new heavens and a new earth.
The former things will not be remembered,
   nor will they come to mind.
But be glad and rejoice forever

in what I will create,
for I will create Jerusalem to be a delight
    and its people a joy. (Isa. 65:17-18)

The wolf and the lamb will feed together,
    and the lion will eat straw like the ox,
    but dust will be the serpent's food.
They will neither harm nor destroy
    on all my holy mountain. (Isa. 65:25)

The creation waits in eager expectation for the sons of God to be revealed. For the creation was subjected to frustration, not by its own choice, but by the will of the one who subjected it, in hope that the creation itself will be liberated from its bondage to decay and brought into the glorious freedom of the children of God. (Rom. 8:19-21)

So will it be with the resurrection of the dead. The body that is sown is perishable, it is raised imperishable; it is sown in dishonour, it is raised in glory; it is sown in weakness, it is raised in power; it is sown a natural body, it is raised a spiritual body. (1 Cor. 15:42-44)

Listen, I tell you a mystery: We will not all sleep, but we will all be changed – in a flash, in the twinkling of an eye, at the last trumpet. For the trumpet will sound, the dead will be raised imperishable, and we will be changed. For the perishable must clothe itself with the imperishable, and the mortal with immortality. When the perishable has been clothed with the imperishable, and the mortal with immortality, then the saying that is written will come true: 'Death has been swallowed up in victory'. (1 Cor. 15:51-54)

And I heard a loud voice from the throne saying, 'Now the dwelling of God is with men, and he will live with them. They will be his people, and God himself will be with them and be their God. He will wipe every tear from their eyes.

There will be no more death or mourning or crying or pain, for the old order of things has passed away.' (Rev. 21:3-4)

I did not see a temple in the city, because the Lord God Almighty and the Lamb are its temple. The city does not need the sun or the moon to shine on it, for the glory of God gives it light, and the Lamb is its lamp. The nations will walk by its light, and the kings of the earth will bring their splendour into it. On no day will its gates ever be shut, for there will be no night there. The glory and honour of the nations will be brought into it. Nothing impure will ever enter it, nor will anyone who does what is shameful or deceitful, but only those whose names are written in the Lamb's book of life. (Rev. 21:22-27)

Then the angel showed me the river of the water of life, as clear as crystal, flowing from the throne of God and of the Lamb down the middle of the great street of the city. On each side of the river stood the tree of life, bearing twelve crops of fruit, yielding its fruit every month. And the leaves of the tree are for the healing of the nations. No longer will there be any curse. The throne of God and of the Lamb will be in the city, and his servants will serve him. They will see his face, and his name will be on their foreheads. There will be no more night. They will not need the light of a lamp or the light of the sun, for the Lord God will give them light. And they will reign for ever and ever. (Rev. 22:1-5)

These verses (and many more besides) describe the new order. The heavens and the earth are renewed; creation is liberated and restored to its former glory; death and decay are banished forever; weak, mortal and perishable bodies are exchanged for strong, immortal and imperishable ones; there is a new Jerusalem, the city where God dwells with His people. It will be a safe and secure place to live; nothing impure will ever reside there. There will be nothing shameful or unjust about life in the new creation.

The parallels with Eden are obvious. Even the tree of life is present, as it was in the Garden, sustaining God's people with its fruit and bringing healing to the nations. The language is poetic and not to be taken too literally (for example, it's hard to envisage how the tree can be on both sides of the river at the same time) but the metaphors conveyed are good ones. Not only is the created order restored and made perfect but God Himself is present and dwells among His people once more. This signals a return to the intimacy of relationship experienced in Eden, where God walked with Adam and Eve in the cool of the day and talked with them directly. But relationships in the new creation will be even better than before because there is no possibility of sin ruining them. There is no more death, or mourning, or crying or pain. God Himself will wipe away every tear from our eyes. The old order of sinful and broken relationships has passed. The new order of restored and perfected relationships has come. But that's not the only metaphor used to describe what life in the new creation will be like.

The marriage of the Lamb

One big difference between the Garden of Eden and the new creation is the presence of the Lamb, the Lamb who was slain. He bears the scars of that sacrifice, as He took God's curse upon Himself so that none of His people would have to suffer it. He is the reason why there is no temple – the place where atonement had been made before, enabling people to be brought back into relationship with God, at least symbolically. Jesus Himself is the true temple and the means by which atonement is actually made for all those whose names are written in the Book of Life. The presence of the Lord Jesus in the new creation ensures that the new order has come and can never be overthrown. He is the promised serpent-crusher, God's anointed King who rules over all and reigns forever...

> Then I looked and heard the voice of many angels, numbering thousands upon thousands, and ten thousand times ten thousand. They encircled the throne and the living creatures and the elders. In a loud voice they sang:
>
> 'Worthy is the Lamb, who was slain,
> > to receive power and wealth and wisdom and strength
> > and honour and glory and praise!'
>
> Then I heard every creature in heaven and on earth and under the earth and on the sea, and all that is in them, singing:
>
> 'To him who sits on the throne and to the Lamb
> > be praise and honour and glory and power, for ever
> > and ever!' (Rev. 5:11-13)

Jesus, the Lamb of God, is at the heart of everything that happens in the new creation. He is the subject of all praise and adoration; He is the one true King whom people will serve gladly for all eternity; He is the source of all justice, holiness, wisdom and peace. He invites His bride to join Him in the wedding banquet to end all wedding banquets! All authority in heaven and on earth was given to Him after the resurrection[33] but it is only now that it is fully seen. Everything we do, everything we are is bound up in Him. He is the perfect King, the perfect Saviour, the perfect Bridegroom...

---

3 See, for example, Matthew 28:18.

'Hallelujah!
For our Lord God Almighty reigns.
Let us rejoice and be glad
and give him glory!
For the wedding of the Lamb has come,
and his bride has made herself ready. (Rev. 19:6-7)

Blessed are those who are invited to the wedding supper of the Lamb! (Rev. 19:9)

Then I saw a new heaven and a new earth, for the first heaven and the first earth had passed away, and there was no longer any sea. I saw the Holy City, the new Jerusalem, coming down out of heaven from God, prepared as a bride beautifully dressed for her husband. (Rev. 21:1-2)

One of the seven angels who had the seven bowls full of the seven last plagues came and said to me, 'Come, I will show you the bride, the wife of the Lamb.' And he carried me away in the Spirit to a mountain great and high, and showed me the Holy City, Jerusalem, coming down out of heaven from God. (Rev. 21:9)

In these verses, the people of God are sometimes described as a bride and then sometimes as a city. The language is very striking, although it's hard to visualise how both can be true in a literal sense. Nevertheless the metaphors speak very powerfully. Christopher Ash, in his book *Married for God*, writes...

The Lamb, the Lord Jesus Christ Himself, is to be married at last. His bride is His people, every believer of all time, corporately to be joined to Him forever in a union of unmixed delight and intimacy. This is a time for joy and amazement... John sees the heavenly Jerusalem, that is the whole new heavens and new earth, the restored and redeemed created order, coming down out of heaven as a city, but not only a city, also a bride, "prepared as a bride adorned for her husband." For this new and restored creation is "the bride, the wife of the Lamb." All the people of God in the new heavens and new earth are the bride of Christ. That is to say, He loves them passionately and they love Him with an answering love.[4]

What these metaphors are trying to portray is the redeemed community of God, living in the presence of God and enjoying Him forever. The marriage imagery shows that it is a covenant relationship, as the Lamb covenants Himself to His bride for all eternity. There is intimacy and delight depicted here and a relational union that can never be separated. The parallels of intimacy within marriage are deliberate – not that there is sexual intimacy in heaven, but that sexual intimacy in human marriage serves as a pointer to something much more significant. Again, Christopher Ash writes...

In that new age their love will be consummated with an enduring delight that the best human marriage can only begin faintly to echo. To put it bluntly, the most climatic and rapturous delight ever experienced in sexual intimacy by a married couple in the history of the human race cannot hold a candle to the delight of that union.[5]

This brings us back to the idea that earthly marriage and sexual intimacy within it are merely pointers to a much greater heavenly reality. This means that we should be careful not to think of earthly marriage as an end in itself, or to think that Christ's love for the church is given as a means of understanding what a husband's love for his wife should be. It actually works the

---

4   Christopher Ash, *Married for God* (IVP, 2007), p. 166.

5   Ibid., p.167.

other way around. Marriage is a God-given means of understanding a far more significant reality that will one day render all earthly marriages redundant...

> Human marriage is not the reality for which Christ and His church provide a sermonic illustration but the reverse. Human marriage is the earthly type, pointing towards the heavenly reality.[6]

So it's heavenly marriage that is the real marriage; the one true and permanent marriage; the goal and end point for all God's people. Earthly marriage is merely a pointer along the way. It's useful, certainly, as it helps us to understand the heavenly marriage, but only ever in a partial sense. When life in the new creation begins, earthly marriage will cease to be important or necessary. Why settle for life in the shadow-lands when reality is all around you?

The perfection of God's design

But what are the implications of all this for God's design? What will life in the new creation be like for men and women who are made in the image of God? What will the perfection of God's design look like? We do not have the complete picture of what it will be like but Scripture does give us a few clues...

Perfect Equality

There is perfect equality. As the equality of relationships within the Godhead continues throughout eternity, so our equality as His image-bearers also continues; but it will be a perfected equality without any possibility of spoiling. Men and women were equal in status, dignity and humanity at the very beginning, but that was all lost at the Fall and the battle for supremacy took over. In the new

---

6   'Marriage' in the *New Dictionary of Biblical Theology* (IVP, 2000), p. 656.

creation however, that equality is restored and perfected so that they remain equal throughout all eternity. They are heirs together of the gracious gift of eternal life. Their inheritance was guaranteed at conversion by the seal of the Holy Spirit. It was kept for them in heaven where it could never perish, spoil or fade, and is delivered, as promised, at the dawn of the new creation...

> And you also were included in Christ when you heard the word of truth, the gospel of your salvation. Having believed, you were marked in him with a seal, the promised Holy Spirit, who is a deposit guaranteeing our inheritance until the redemption of those who are God's possession – to the praise of his glory. (Eph. 1:13-14)

> Praise be to the God and Father of our Lord Jesus Christ! In his great mercy he has given us new birth into a living hope through the resurrection of Jesus Christ from the dead, and into an inheritance that can never perish, spoil or fade – kept in heaven for you... (1 Pet. 1:3-4)

> He said to me: 'It is done. I am the Alpha and the Omega, the Beginning and the End. To him who is thirsty I will give to drink without cost from the spring of the water of life. He who overcomes will inherit all this, and I will be his God and he will be my son.' (Rev. 21:6-7)

And in the new creation there is nothing to threaten this equality – there is no competitiveness or injustice, no selfish ambition or petty rivalry, no envy or one-up-man-ship. There is no battle for supremacy as Jesus Himself is the supreme authority and men and women are His humble servants. There is nothing impure or shameful or unjust about our existence in the new creation. There is perfect equality.

Perfect Diversity

But there is also perfect diversity. As the diversity within the Godhead continues throughout eternity, so our diversity as His image-bearers also continues; but it will be a perfected diversity without any possibility of spoiling. We are equal but also individually unique as each person is given a new name by the Lord Jesus...

> To him who overcomes, I will give some of the hidden manna. I will also give him a white stone with a new name written on it, known only to him who receives it. (Rev. 2:17)

There is a rich diversity of work in the new creation. Some will build houses, others will plant vineyards and still others will rule cities, and it seems as though the amount of responsibility we have in the new creation will, in some way, reflect the degree to which we have brought honour to the Lord Jesus in this life...

> They will build houses and dwell in them;
>   they will plant vineyards and eat their fruit.
> No longer will they build houses and others live in them,
>   or plant and others eat.
> For as the days of a tree,
>   so will be the days of my people;
> My chosen ones will long enjoy
>   the works of their hands. (Isa. 65:21-22)

> 'Then [the king] sent for the servants to whom he had given the money, in order to find out what they had gained with it.

> The first one came and said, "Sir, your mina has earned ten more." "Well done, my good servant!" his master replied. "Because you have been trustworthy in a very small matter, take charge of ten cities."

The second came and said, "Sir, your mina has earned five more." His master answered, "You take charge of five cities." (Luke 19:15-19)

Some people are a little uncomfortable with this notion of 'rewards' in heaven, but there is evidence in the Bible to suggest that we can expect degrees of reward in eternity depending on how we have lived for the Lord Jesus here on earth.[7] Of course, in the shadow-lands our sinful hearts and minds find it hard to understand how this can be possible without envy and petty rivalries creeping in, but in the new creation our hearts and minds will be renewed and these sinful thoughts a thing of the past.

Jonathan Edwards made this point well when he wrote…

It will be no damp to the happiness of those who have lower degrees of happiness and glory, that there are others advanced in glory above them; for all shall be perfectly happy, everyone shall be perfectly satisfied…. Those who are not so high in glory as others, will not envy those that are higher, but they will have such a great, and strong, and pure love for them, that they will rejoice in their superior happiness… so instead of having a damp to their own happiness, it will add to it. [8]

There is a rich diversity of good work to be done in the new creation. The futility of work in the shadow-lands gives way to fruitful and useful work in the new

---

7   See, for example, Matthew 5:12, Matthew 6:1-6, 1 Corinthians 3:10-15, 2 John 8 and Revelation 11:18.
8   Jonathan Edwards, *The Works of Jonathan Edwards*, Vol. 2 (Banner of Truth, 1974) quoted in John Piper's *Let the Nations Be Glad!* (IVP), p. 88.

creation.[9] To what extent these roles will be gender specific remains to be seen. There is no suggestion in Scripture that women won't take charge of cities alongside men but the Lord Jesus is King and everything will be done in full and joyful submission to Him.

Perfect Unity

There is also perfect unity. As the unity of the Godhead continues into eternity, so the unity of believers will also continue; but it will be a perfected unity without any possibility of spoiling. Our union in Christ will be complete and fully mature…

> As a prisoner for the Lord, then, I urge you to live a life worthy of the calling you have received. Be completely humble and gentle; be patient, bearing with one another in love. Make every effort to keep the unity of the Spirit through the bond of peace. There is one body and one Spirit – just as you were called to one hope when you were called – one Lord, one faith, one baptism; one God and Father of all, who is over all and through all and in all. (Eph. 4:1-6)

> It was he who gave some to be apostles, some to be prophets, some to be evangelists, and some to be pastors and teachers, to prepare God's people for works of service, so that the body of Christ may be built up until we all reach unity in the faith and in the knowledge of the Son of God and become mature, attaining to the whole measure of the fullness of Christ.

> Then we will no longer be infants, tossed back and forth by the waves, and blown here and there by every wind of teaching and by the cunning and craftiness of men in their deceitful scheming. Instead, speaking the truth in love, we will in all things grow up into him who is the Head, that is,

---

9   See, for example, Isaiah 65:23.

Christ. From him the whole body, joined and held together
by every supporting ligament, grows and builds itself up in
love, as each part does its work. (Eph. 4:11-16)

Our unity with Christ will be complete. There will be
unity in the faith and in the knowledge of the Christ.
The body of Christ will attain the whole measure of the
fullness of Christ and be mature, each member doing
their God-given work in love. The ministry of the Word
will be completed and God's people fully prepared for
life in the new creation. We won't need church leaders
any longer to teach us the Word of God, because it will
be written on all our hearts...

> 'This is the covenant I will make with the house of Israel
>   after that time,' declares the LORD.
> 'I will put my law in their minds
>   and write it on their hearts.
> I will be their God,
>   and they will be my people.
> No longer will a man teach his neighbour,
>   or a man his brother, saying, "Know the LORD,"
> because they will all know me,
>   from the least of them to the greatest,'
>   declares the LORD. (Jer. 31:33-34)

That's not to say that the Word of God won't have any
relevance in the new creation, far from it, but living by
it will be second nature. We won't need Scripture to
teach, rebuke, correct and train us as we do now because
our training will be over. Our union with Christ will be
complete and we will be fully mature.

And there will be no crafty serpent to tempt us into
disobeying the Word of God. Our sinful natures will
be finally put to death so that nothing can threaten the

unity we have with Christ. There will be no divisions, no doctrinal differences, no factions or tribal segregation. The body of Christ will be united with Christ, who is its head, and every member will live in perfect unity. We will always conduct ourselves in a manner worthy of the gospel and grieving the Spirit will be a thing of the past. There will be perfect unity.

Perfect Order

And lastly, there will be perfect order. As the order within the Godhead continues into eternity, so the order of believers will also continue; but it will be a perfected order without any possibility of spoiling. The marriage of the Lord Jesus with His bride, the church, will consummate their order and their union once and for all…

> Wives, submit to your husbands as to the Lord. For the husband is the head of the wife as Christ is the head of the church, his body, of which he is the Saviour. Now as the church submits to Christ, so also wives should submit to their husbands in everything.
>
> Husbands, love your wives, just as Christ loved the church and gave himself up for her to make her holy, cleansing her by the washing with water through the word, and to present her to himself as a radiant church, without stain or wrinkle or any other blemish, but holy and blameless. In this same way, husbands ought to love their wives as their own bodies. He who loves his wife loves himself. After all, no one ever hated his own body, but he feeds and cares for it, just as Christ does the church – for we are members of his body. 'For this reason a man will leave his father and mother and be united to his wife, and the two will become one flesh.' This is a profound mystery – but I am talking about Christ and the church. (Eph. 5:22-32)

Of course, there will be no human marriage in the new creation so the gender roles within marriage no longer apply and cease to be relevant. The helpful pointers for life in the shadow-lands give way, once more, to the reality of life in the new creation. The bridegroom lovingly cherishes His bride, having already given Himself up for her and made her holy; and the bride of Christ humbly submits to her Lord in everything. There is total trust, joyful surrender and the end to all our longings.

And there will be no crafty serpent to tempt us to overthrow this order. The rule of the Lord Jesus will be established for all eternity and His people will live in humble praise and submission for all eternity...

In my vision at night I looked, and there before me was one like a son of man, coming with the clouds of heaven. He approached the Ancient of Days and was led into his presence. He was given authority, glory and sovereign power; all peoples, nations and men of every language worshiped him. His dominion is an everlasting dominion that will not pass away, and his kingdom is one that will never be destroyed. (Dan. 7:13-14)

After this I looked and there before me was a great multitude that no one could count, from every nation, tribe, people and language, standing before the throne and in front of the Lamb. They were wearing white robes and were holding palm branches in their hands. And they cried out in a loud voice:

'Salvation belongs to our God,
    who sits on the throne,
and to the Lamb.' (Rev. 7:9-10)

'The kingdom of the world has become
    the kingdom of our Lord and of his Christ,
and he will reign for ever and ever.' (Rev. 11:15)

Perfect equality, perfect diversity, perfect unity and perfect order. These are just some of the attributes to our life in the new creation that help us to understand, at least to some extent, what the perfection of God's design will be like. But what does this all mean for us today? What does an understanding of what life will be like in the new creation mean for those who are still living in the shadow-lands?

[1] Don't expect too much from this life

First of all, we should be careful not to expect too much from this life. This life is not the real deal; there is more to come. Everything we consider valuable in this life will be superseded in the life that is to come. Every moment of happiness, every moment of laughter and joy will be a vague and distant memory in the new creation. Nothing we enjoy in this life now can even begin to compare with what life will be like then. Nothing.

Not only that but we would do well to remember that this life is supposed to be full of frustrations, trials, difficulties and pain. Life in the here and now is not as it should be because it is under the curse of God. But one day that curse will be gone and the whole of creation will be liberated from its bondage to death and decay. Many of life's disappointments come when we expect too much from this world and think we should be able to find total fulfilment in the here and now. We can't protect ourselves from the frustrations and trials that come. They are often God's means of growing our faith and establishing godly character.[10]

Jesus taught His disciples to persevere to the end and not give up in the face of difficulties and trials...

---

10   See, for example, Romans 5:3-5, James 1:2-4 and 1 Peter 1:6-7.

'The seed is the word of God. Those along the path are the ones who hear, and then the devil comes and takes away the word from their hearts, so that they may not believe and be saved. Those on the rock are the ones who receive the word with joy when they hear it, but they have no root. They believe for a while, but in the time of testing they fall away. The seed that fell among thorns stands for those who hear, but as they go on their way they are choked by life's worries, riches and pleasures, and they do not mature. But the seed on good soil stands for those with a noble and a good heart, who hear the word, retain it, and by persevering produce a crop.' (Luke 8:11-15)

The things that cause people to give up are times of testing and the worries, riches and pleasures of this life, but all of these stem from a misunderstanding of what this world is like. Life in the new creation will be wonderful but it hasn't started yet. We must be careful not to expect too much from this life – from our jobs, our families, our homes, even our Christian service. Perfection will come, but not in this life.

[2] Remember that earthly pointers are not ends in themselves

Secondly, we should remember that the pointers to life in the new creation are not ends in themselves. Marriage and family life are wonderful gifts from the Lord but they are not the be all and end all of our existence. Those who are married need to be careful not to substitute the shadow-lands for the reality that is to come. Similarly, those who are single but long to be married need to have a right perspective on what human marriage points to. Whether married or single, we need to remind ourselves that the blessings of life in the new creation are better than the blessings of marriage and children in the here and now. There will come a time when human marriage and family life will cease to be important or even relevant. We should be careful not to miss out on what they are pointing to.

John Piper, in answering the question 'wouldn't it be better to have both the blessings of marriage and the blessings of heaven,' helpfully points out that…

> There are two answers to that question. One is that you will find out someday, and better to learn it now, that the blessings of being in Christ in heaven are so far superior to the blessings of being married and raising children that asking this question will be like asking, wouldn't it be better to have the ocean and also the thimbleful? But that's not the answer you wanted. So here is another one: Marriage and singleness both present us with unique trials and unique opportunities for our sanctification – our preparation for heaven. There will be rewards for each. Which is greater will not depend on whether you were married or single, but on how you responded to each.[11]

[3] Invest in eternity

The third implication is a natural extension of this, namely, that we need to invest in eternity. Nothing of our physical existence in this life will last forever. We should be careful therefore not to invest in the wrong things. It's not wrong to work hard at a career, buy a house, settle down and have a family, watch what we eat, take care of our bodies and so on. Just so long as we remember that careers come to an end, houses deteriorate, children grow up, health declines and bodies fall apart. What does last into eternity is our

---

11   John Piper, *This Momentary Marriage* (IVP, 2009), p. 113.

spiritual existence – the development of godly character, the love we have for God's people, the relationship we have with the Lord and our joyful service of Him. These are the kinds of things we should invest in. The New Testament makes this quite clear...

Do not be deceived: God cannot be mocked. A man reaps what he sows. The one who sows to please his sinful nature, from that nature will reap destruction; the one who sows to please the Spirit, from the Spirit will reap eternal life. Let us not become weary in doing good, for at the proper time we will reap a harvest if we do not give up. Therefore, as we have opportunity, let us do good to all people, especially to those who belong to the family of believers. (Gal. 6:7-10)

You are all sons of the light and sons of the day. We do not belong to the night or to the darkness. So then, let us not be like others, who are asleep, but let us be alert and self-controlled. For those who sleep, sleep at night and those who get drunk, get drunk at night. But since we belong to the day, let us be self-controlled, putting on faith and love as a breastplate, and the hope of salvation as a helmet. For God did not appoint us to suffer wrath but to receive salvation through our Lord Jesus Christ. He died for us so that, whether we are awake or asleep, we may live together with him. Therefore encourage one another and build each other up, just as in fact you are doing. (1 Thess. 5:5-11)

Now that you have purified yourselves by obeying the truth so that you have sincere love for your brothers, love one another deeply, from the heart. For you have been born again, not of perishable seed, but of imperishable, through the living and enduring word of God. For,

'All men are like grass,
    and all their glory is like the flowers of the field;

the grass withers and the flowers fall,
    but the word of the Lord stands forever.'

And this is the word that was preached to you. Therefore, rid yourselves of all malice and all deceit, hypocrisy, envy, and slander of every kind. Like newborn babies, crave pure spiritual milk, so that by it you may grow up in your salvation, now that you have tasted that the Lord is good. (1 Pet. 1:22 – 2:3)

[4] Long for heaven

And lastly, we should long for heaven. Heaven awaits. Life in the shadow-lands will one day give way to life in the reality of the new creation. Everything will be restored and perfected. Nothing of our old fallen existence will remain. Our work will be perfected, our character will be perfected, our relationships will be perfected. And it will be even better than before – with fruit from the tree of life to sustain us and at the heart of our existence, the greatest bridegroom of them all. He is the reason why we are there. He is the One who saved us, who nurtured us, cherished us and brought us home to be with Him forever. Everything we do will be inextricably bound up with Him. He is the One we will exist for. He is the One to whom all honour and glory and praise will be due. He is the One we will serve and joyfully submit to. Nothing we experience here on earth will compare with our life and existence then. I hope you're looking forward to it – I know that I am.

Knowing what lies ahead gives us great hope in the face of present difficulties and trials. Life in the shadow-lands is painful and frustrating and full of disappointment. Three days ago I heard that a dear friend of mine has inoperable cancer. Her treatment options are very limited and while the doctors have said they will do everything they can to prolong her life, it does look as though she is now terminally ill. It's a terribly sad situation but it's not hopeless. My friend is a Christian and she's looking forward to heaven. She said to me over the phone this week, 'Carrie, I know whatever the short-term future holds, it will be nothing compared to what is to come afterwards. The Lord has gone ahead and has promised to prepare a room in His Father's house for each one of us. I think mine is nearly ready.'

The Apostle Paul said much the same thing…

> Therefore we do not lose heart. Though outwardly we are wasting away, yet inwardly we are being renewed day by day. For our light and momentary troubles are achieving for us an eternal glory that far outweighs them all. So we fix our eyes not on what is seen, but on what is unseen. For what is seen is temporary, but what is unseen is eternal. (2 Cor. 4:16-18)

DISCUSSION QUESTIONS FOR GROUPS/INDIVIDUALS

1. To what extent do we think of earthly marriage as an end in itself rather than a pointer to something much more significant?

2. How does the metaphor of the heavenly banquet help us to understand what life in the new creation will be like? What are the implications for the church as we prepare to be His bride?

3. What will the perfection of God's design look like? How much can we enjoy these blessings now?

4. To what extent are we expecting too much from this world? How can we invest more in eternity?

5. How can we encourage each other to long for heaven?

Conclusion

When the Lord Jesus returns, will He find good order in our families, our workplaces and our churches? Or, to put it another way, how well will we be modelling God's image and His design for men and women in the particular contexts that He has placed us? To what extent will we be demonstrating the equality, diversity, unity and order that are found at the very heart of His being? This is the pattern for our design as men and women; this is what was lost when Adam and Eve rebelled against the Lord God who had created them; this is what the Lord Jesus restored as He died on the cross and secured our eternal redemption; this is what He looks for in His people, as they seek to reflect God's image in their families, their workplaces and their churches.

But what would good order look like for Sally, the 35-year-old lawyer, who is wondering if she really wants to become a partner in her law firm and stay there for the next thirty years? She is undoubtedly very able and could have a long and very successful career – but her competitiveness, especially with her male colleagues, isn't helping her to honour the Lord in the workplace and may be the cause of her inability to forge lasting relationships with men outside of work. Of course, there is no guarantee that a change in attitude and behaviour will suddenly lead to marriage and the fulfilment of her dream of 'having it all'. The Lord may have different plans for her. But understanding that men and women are equal and yet have different roles to play in the family and the church may make her working relationships a little easier. The Lord is certainly more concerned about how she fights the natural tendency she has to control and manipulate men than whether she chalks up an impressive career in law.

What would good order look like for Denise and Simon? Their career choices seem to be having an unhelpful impact on their marriage and family life. It's not that Denise cannot work outside the home, but her chosen career, and in particular the amount of travelling it involves, is having a negative effect on her children, who are beginning to feel neglected, and on her husband, who is in danger of being emasculated. If Denise and Simon were to better understand the different roles the Lord has given them in marriage and the family, and embrace them, the relationships they have with each other and with their children would be transformed. These changes would also mitigate the guilt that Denise feels when she's away from home; guilt that, if left unchecked, will develop into full-blown regret when the children have flown the nest and left home. The Lord is certainly more concerned about the ministry she has as a wife and mother than how many international clients she visits on her travels.

And what about our churches? What would good order look like for them? Surely, the Lord will expect to find men and women working together as partners in the cause of the gospel, aware of the unique roles they are to play in the teaching, training, and modelling of the Christian life to younger disciples? Surely, He will expect to see some of the men taking the lead and exercising authority in formal teaching roles, with everyone else, both men and women, serving the body of Christ and seeking to build it up in more informal ways? The trouble is, the way our society is going means that our churches are becoming more and more feminised – with dwindling numbers of men in leadership roles and fewer men being won for Christ than ever before. We desperately need to encourage more men into positions of leadership; and that means we need to pray for godly older men who can teach and encourage and disciple them. It also means that godly older women need to be prepared to hang back and not dominate church councils, prayer meetings or small group Bible studies. We are all losers if the church isn't encouraging godly men to take the initiative and lead their families and the local church as God intended.

I take it that we are all work in progress, but if the Lord is to find good order in our families, our workplaces and our churches, then we still have a long way to go. The battle with sin is very real and the world, the flesh and the devil will do everything they can to prevent us from living ordered lives that are pleasing to the Lord. Society will encourage us to look after number one and fight for our rights; our sinful natures will entice us to manipulate and control everyone around us; and the evil one will feed us the lies that are behind every act of rebellion and disorderly conduct. So the battle with

sin is very real, but progress is possible because of the
death of Christ and the gift of His Spirit. We do not
have to live as we once did. The power of sin and death
and hell was defeated at the cross of our Lord Jesus
Christ and we are free to live a new life in Him. The
Spirit is given as a deposit, guaranteeing that we now
belong to Christ and will one day inherit all that has
been promised. But He also works within us and is the
means by which we can live lives that are honouring to
the Lord.

As God's chosen people, we have different roles to
play within a whole range of different contexts. Sometimes those contexts require us to take the initiative and
lead the people in our care; sometimes those contexts
require us to humbly submit to those in authority over
us. Whatever our situation, the Lord Jesus understands
it and is able to identify and sympathise with all our
weaknesses. He is the perfect model of both humble
submission and sacrificial leadership, as He humbly
submitted to His Father's will in the Garden of Gethsemane and sacrificially led the church by giving Himself up for her when He died on the cross. He knows
what it is like to be treated harshly and unjustly, but
He remained obedient to His Father's will and was gloriously vindicated at the resurrection. He was tempted
in every way that we are, yet never sinned, and because
of this we can approach the throne of grace with confidence, so that we might receive mercy and find grace to
help us in our time of need (Heb. 4:15-16).

So, whatever situation we may be facing, whether
it's the battle with our own sinful hearts or the injustice
of external circumstances, the Lord expects us to
behave as He did and to reflect the image of God in
a broken and disordered world. He longs for us to

model the equality of men and women created in His image, to embrace the diversity of roles that stem from His very being, and to rejoice in the unity and order that come from lives lived in submission to His will. This is how the image of God is to be demonstrated. This is how God's design for men and women works out in practice in a world that doesn't understand, embrace, or model it, and, as a result, suffers all the associated consequences. We live in a broken, fallen, and disordered world, but it is not a world without hope. One day our life in the shadow-lands will give way to the reality of life in the new creation – where everything will be made new. Nothing we experience in the here and now can compare with our life and existence then. And at the centre of it all will be the Lord Jesus Christ – risen, ascended and glorified.

May the lives we live here in the shadow-lands anticipate and long for all that life in the new creation will bring. May our families, our churches and our workplaces reflect something of the equality, diversity, unity and order that we will perfectly experience then. May we rejoice in the privilege of being made in the image of God and, in our relationships together, may we seek to reflect that image in appropriate ways that bring honour to His name. May we learn to serve the God who loves us, and forever rejoice in the knowledge that He has made us different by design.

Bibliography

Alexander, T. Desmond and Rosner, B. S. (eds.). *New Dictionary of Biblical Theology* (IVP, 2000).

Ash, Christopher. *Married for God* (IVP, 2007).

Chester, Tim. *Delighting in the Trinity* (Monarch, 2005).

Dante, Tori with Fisher, Julia. *Our Little Secret* (Hodder & Stoughton, 2nd edition, 2006).

Grudem, Wayne. *Evangelical Feminism and Biblical Truth* (Apollos, 2004).

— 'How different views on gender affect other areas of life' (*Evangelicals Now*, November 2000).

— *Systematic Theology* (IVP, 1994).

— 'Gender Distinctives' (*Council for Biblical Manhood and Womanhood Conference, Oxford,* June 2002).

Henry, Matthew. *Commentary on the Whole Bible*, 6 volumes (Marshall Pickering, 1961).

Jackman, David. *Spirit of Truth* (Christian Focus, 2006).

Jeffery, Steve; Ovey, Mike; and Sach, Andrew. *Pierced for our Transgressions* (IVP, 2007).

Leeman, Jonathan. 'Understanding and honouring distinctness' (9 Marks eJournal, July/August 2010, Volume 7, Issue 3).

— 'Why complementarianism is crucial to discipleship' (9 Marks eJournal, July/August 2010, Volume 7, Issue 3).

McGrath, Alister. *The Triune God* quoted in *Almighty God* by the Co-Mission Initiative (B&B Press, 2008).

Murrow, David. *Why Men Hate Going to Church* (Nelson Books, 2005).

Pease, Allan and Barbara. *Why Men Don't Listen and Women Can't Read Maps* (Orion Press, 2001).

Piper, John. *Let the Nations be Glad!* (IVP, 2003).

— *This Momentary Marriage* (IVP, 2009).

Piper, John. & Grudem, Wayne. *Recovering Biblical Manhood and Womanhood* (Crossway, 1991).

Sayers, Dorothy L. *Are Women Human?* (Eerdmanns, 1971).

Spencer, Caroline. 'Christian women and corporate leadership' (City Bible Forum, Sydney, April 2010).

Stott, John R. W. *The Contemporary Christian* (IVP, 1992).

Stott, John R. W. *The Cross of Christ* (IVP, 1986).

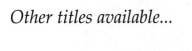

Other titles available...

THE
ENVY
OF *Eve*

FINDING CONTENTMENT IN
A COVETOUS WORLD

MELISSA B. KRUGER

ISBN 978-1-84550-775-6

The Envy of Eve
Finding contentment in a covetous world

MELISSA KRUGER

Melissa Kruger teaches from Scripture that covetousness has taken hold when we do not have the right desires in the right way. She encourages women to check the object of our desires, as well as our motives, means and attitudes.

The Envy of Eve guides readers to understand how desires grow into covetousness and what happens when this sin takes power in our hearts. Covetousness chokes out the fruit of the spirit in our lives, allowing discontentment to bloom. The key to overcoming is to get to the root of our problem: unbelief—a mistrust of God's sovereignty and goodness.

> *...grounded in the Scriptures, the Reformed confessions, and her own wise diagnosis, reflections, and helpful treatment ... I commend this fine, new book... with a prayer that we all read and follow her Biblical counsel to fully understand the condition we are in and flee quickly to the One who truly satisfies our deepest longings and our true desires.*

> Michael A. Milton,
> Chancellor, Reformed Theological Seminary,
> Charlotte, North Carolina

Melissa Kruger serves as Women's Ministry Coordinator at Uptown Church in Charlotte, North Carolina, where her husband, Mike, serves as an Associate Pastor. Melissa and Mike are parents of three children—Emma, John, and Kate.

Diana Lynn Severance

Feminine Threads

Women in the Tapestry of Christian History

ISBN 978-1-84550-640-7

Feminine Threads
Women in the Tapestry of Christian History

DIANA LYNN SEVERANCE

From commoner to queen, the women in this book embraced the freedom and the power of the Gospel in making their unique contributions to the unfolding of history. Wherever possible, the women here speak for themselves, from their letters, diaries or published works. The true story of women in Christian history inspires, challenges and demonstrates the grace of God producing much fruit throughout time.

> *Feminine Threads is a must-read for men and women alike, but especially so for young women who need to have a clear view of the contributions that women before them have made to the Christian faith.*
>
> Carolyn McCulley
> Conference Speaker and Author of
> *Radical Womanhood: Feminine Faith in a Feminist World,*
> Arlington, Virginia

Diana Severance is an historian with broad experience teaching in universities and seminaries.

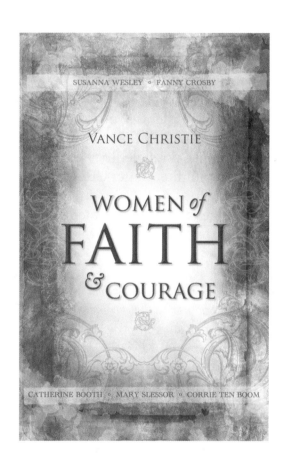

SUSANNA WESLEY ○ FANNY CROSBY

VANCE CHRISTIE

WOMEN *of*

FAITH

& COURAGE

CATHERINE BOOTH ○ MARY SLESSOR ○ CORRIE TEN BOOM

ISBN 978-1-84550-686-5

Women of Faith and Courage

VANCE CHRISTIE

Through some of the best-loved heroines of the Christian faith, God's glory is manifest as He accomplishes significant things through imperfect people. In *Women of Faith* readers discover the remarkable stories of Susanna Wesley, Fanny Crosby, Catherine Booth, Mary Slessor and Corrie ten Boom. Their lives spanned three centuries and their circumstances were each very different, but steadfast faith and courage is the constant resounding theme for each.

In *Women of Faith* engaging narratives with rich historical detail reveal the uncommon faithfulness of these five women in evangelism, missions pioneering, ministries of compassion and the nurturing of their own families. Their giftedness, resilience and compassion shine through, modeling devotion to Christ and sacrificial service in His kingdom.

Across the pages of this book, the legacy of these women lives on to inspire and instruct contemporary believers-in living all of life for the glory of God.

He has written each life story in such a vibrant way, truly making each of the five women come alive.

Helen Roseveare,
Author, Speaker, Belfast, Northern Ireland

Vance Christie is a pastor and author best known for vivid retelling of missionary stories. He lives in Aurora, Nebraska and has previously written for the 'Heroes of the Faith' series.

Christian Focus Publications
publishes books for all ages

Our mission statement –

STAYING FAITHFUL
In dependence upon God we seek to impact the world through literature faithful to His infallible Word, the Bible. Our aim is to ensure that the Lord Jesus Christ is presented as the only hope to obtain forgiveness of sin, live a useful life and look forward to heaven with Him.

REACHING OUT
Christ's last command requires us to reach out to our world with His gospel. We seek to help fulfil that by publishing books that point people towards Jesus and help them develop a Christ-like maturity. We aim to equip all levels of readers for life, work, ministry and mission.

Books in our adult range are published in three imprints:

Christian Focus contains popular works including biographies, commentaries, basic doctrine and Christian living. Our children's books are also published in this imprint.

Mentor focuses on books written at a level suitable for Bible College and seminary students, pastors, and other serious readers. The imprint includes commentaries, doctrinal studies, examination of current issues and church history.

Christian Heritage contains classic writings from the past.

Christian Focus Publications Ltd,
Geanies House, Fearn, Ross-shire,
IV20 1TW, Scotland, United Kingdom.
www.christianfocus.com